JAPANESE FAIRY TALES II

BAKEMONODERA

JAPANESE FAIRY TALES
II

Adapted by
J. ROBERT MAGEE

YOHAN PUBLICATIONS, INC.

JAPANESE FAIRY TALES II

First printing September 1995

Copyright © 1995 by J. Robert Magee

All rights reserved. This book, or parts thereof, must not be reproduced in any form without permission of the publisher.

Illustrated by
KAZUMASA MIYAMOTO
HIROKO KANZAKI

YOHAN PUBLICATIONS, INC.
14-9, Okubo 3-chome, Shinjuku-ku, Tokyo, Japan.

Printed in Japan

Contents

Tengu no Kakuremino—The Tengu and his Robe of Invisibility 1

Tsuru no Ongaeshi—The Gift of the Crane 17

Ubasuteyama—The Mountain of Exile for the Elderly 28

Warashibe Chōja—A Fortune from Straw 41

Furuya no Mori—The Wolf and the Horse Thief 57

The Racing Rice Cake of Fortune 69

Shitakiri Suzume—The Tongueless Sparrow 87

Sannin Kyōdai—The Three Brothers 104

Bakemonodera—The Monk and the Evil Temple 129

Kachi-kachi-yama 137

Note: Japanese folk tales are full of stories where animal transform themselves into human form. Sometimes these are evil animals changing shape to hurt humans, ande sometimes these are good animals with more noble intentions.

Tengu no Kakuremino — The Tengu and his Robe of Invisibility

Long ago, in a small town that has since grown into a great city, there lived a boy named Hiro. Hiro was very clever, but he devoted most of his energies to avoiding work and study.

Hiro's town was in a part of the country frequented by goblins known as tengu. Tengu were known for their long noses and the mischievous pranks they played on humans. Sometimes a tengu's pranks caused great harm and injury, destroying whole towns; sometimes their antics were simply harmless practical jokes. They were helped in their deeds by one very valuable item: a magic robe that made the wearer completely invisible.

One day while his parents thought he was at school, Hiro decided he was going to get his own robe of invisibility. He went to a bamboo grove near a hill that overlooked the town, and there he down cut a slender branch of the wood. He trimmed the branch until he had a stick about three feet in length. Then, he took the stick with him to the top of the hill, where he climbed the tallest tree he could find.

He climbed to top of the tree, where he put

the bamboo to his eye and cried out in a loud voice, "Wooo, Edo's burning. Smoke everywhere. How awful."

Then he turned a bit to his left and called out, "Ah, Osaka looks quiet today."

He turned back to his right a bit and called out again, "A battle! A battle in Aki! How exciting!"

The wind carried Hiro's voice to the ears of a tengu napping under a tree at the edge of the forest.

"What's this?" said the tengu. "This sounds interesting!"

The tengu, wearing his coat of invisibility, ran to the base of Hiro's tree, where he listened to the boy continue to describe scenes from far away parts of Japan.

The tengu, who had long dreamt of seeing Edo, Kyoto, Nara and other great cities of Japan, was excited with what he heard. He made himself visible and called to the boy.

"Hello up there."

Hiro looked down. The tengu was a horrible monster, whose appearance would frighten most ordinary men. But Hiro steeled himself to the challenge. He knew any sign of fear would invite the tengu to attack. He calmly replied, "Hello down there."

The tengu, somewhat taken aback at not frightening the boy, called back. "I say hello up there," he called, hoping the boy would realize he was talking to a legendary tengu, a mysterious beast that could wreak all sorts of havoc on mankind.

"I heard you the first time," the boy called down again.

"I'm a tengu."

"Hello."

"A tengu, you know. A ferocious, mayhem-wreaking monster."

"Yes."

"Well?"

"My name is Hiro."

"Right," said the tengu. Frightening the boy was not working, so the tengu turned to diplomacy. "What's that you have there?" he asked.

Hiro, sensing the tengu had changed his tactics, found his confidence returning. "This is the stick of sight. I can see any place I choose just by looking through this stick." he said. To illustrate, he raised the stick to his eye and said, "See? There's a ship sinking off the Satsuma coast. And Edo's burning."

"No," replied the tengu. "I don't see. I can't see these things."

"Aha. That's because you don't have the stick."

"Yes. But if you gave it to me, I could see what was happening there."

"True," answered the boy, "but you're a tengu aren't you? I don't mean to be rude, but tengu aren't really known for their trustworthiness, are they?"

"That? Where do you hear things like that?" asked the monster, feigning great hurt. "What are they teaching in your schools these days? True, there are a few bad apples, but most of us are pretty straight arrows, you know."

"Well, I'm not sure. The stick of seeing is a very valuable thing. You don't come across one every day. It's the most valuable thing I have."

"Hmm," murmured the tengu. "This is the most valuable thing I have," he said, pointing to a ragged, tattered old coat.

"That?" asked Hiro.

"This is the coat of invisibility. Just watch." The tengu slipped the tattered coat over his shoulders and winked out of sight. Then he faded back into view, holding the coat in his hands. "Pretty powerful, huh?"

Hiro tried to sound unimpressed. "Well, it is

a nice toy, but it's nothing like the stick of seeing. What do you hate most in all the world?"

"What do I hate most? Onions. Why? What do you hate most in all the world?"

"Rice cakes and candy. Oh, and those little buns filled with sweet bean paste? I really hate those — more than anything."

The tengu was growing impatient. "Fine, fine. Now, about the stick of sight. Let me hold it — just for a little while — and I'll let you hold the coat of invisibility. Okay?"

"Well, I guess that's okay. But just for a little while."

"Agreed."

Hiro jumped down from the tree. He handed the stick to the tengu and at the same moment took from him his coat of invisibility. The tengu looked at the bamboo stick, then turned to the south and held it to his eye as Hiro slipped into the coat.

"Hey, how does this thing work?" called the tengu, but the boy was nowhere in sight. Not realizing he had been deceived, the tengu tried looking in a different direction, then looking through the other end of the stick.

"Am I holding this the right way?" he asked, but Hiro had long since made his escape and raced back to the town.

When he returned to town, Hiro took off the robe and slipped it into his pack. Then he went to the farmers and bought all the onions he could find. He went back to his house and put the onions all around his house, hanging clusters from doorways, cutting them and dropping slices around the garden and the gate to his home.

The tengu soon discovered he had been fooled. He broke the stick over a scaly knee and stormed into the town, looking for the boy. He tracked the boy to his house by his scent, and flexed his muscles in anticipation of the thrashing he was going to give the little boy. But as he entered the gate, his sensitive nose was overwhelmed by the stink of onions. He tried to enter the gate, but he could not overcome the horrible onion smell. His mouth was as dry as sand. With

each step he took into the compound his eyes watered until he could go no further. Defeated, he retreated to the gateway to the garden.

"Two can play this game, boy!" yelled the

tengu. He used his magic to conjure up a bag full of rice cakes, candy and jam-filled buns. "Take that! he cried, throwing a handful of candy through Hiro's window. A barrage of sweetcakes and other treats continued until the tengu spied the boy sitting happily eating a jambun.

Realizing he had been fooled yet again, the tengu became even angrier than before. "Boy!" he raged. "These onions will rot within a couple of days. When the stink fades, I'll still be here, waiting for you."

The voice boomed through Hiro's home and frightened him. Even with the coat of invisibility, he was trapped. Even if he left the house, the gateway, where the angry tengu stood waiting, was the only way out of the garden.

But the tengu's booming voice reached more ears than he intended. The villagers of the town heard the goblin's threat and took up arms. Soon, every man in the village was armed and on his way to Hiro's home.

The tengu, wasn't worried. "Foolish humans," he thought. They can't hurt me if they can't find me, and I have my coat of — No!"

The tengu, of course, did not have his coat of invisibility. The first villagers to reach Hiro's home were startled to see a tengu in their village. Few had ever seen such a creature, as most tengu were invisible. But when ten more villagers, then ten more, then ten more arrived on the scene, the first villagers shed their fear and grew bolder.

"A tengu! Get him!" they shouted, waving poles, rakes and other weapons.

The tengu realized he was no match for an entire village — especially when everyone could see him. He turned and ran from the village. The villagers, angry and excited with the thought of taking their revenge for years of tengu pranks and mayhem, followed the beast, and did not stop until they had chased him to the border with the neighboring province.

At the border, the tengu thought of asking the tengu of the province for help. On second thought, though, he realized that any tengu who allowed himself to be tricked out of his coat of invisibility would probably be exiled from the tengu world. He had no choice but to continue his flight.

Meanwhile, the villagers from Hiro's province alerted their neighbors to the presence of the tengu. The neighbors joined the chase, following the tengu until they came to the border of another province. There they passed the chase on to yet another group of villagers, and the pursuit continued in this fashion until the tengu was far from Hiro's village.

Once the tengu had been chased from the land, Hiro put on the coat of invisibility and set out on the first of many adventures. First, he went to the village market to see what mischief he could cause there.

On the road to the market, he found Taro,

the neighborhood bully, fighting with one of Hiro's friends. To use the word "fighting" is misleading — Taro was older and much bigger than Hiro and his friends, and Taro could easily best them in a fight. Hiro's friend had done something to displease the bully, and Taro was sitting on top of him, rubbing his face in the dirt.

Normally, Hiro would have shied away from any sort of trouble with Taro — he had tasted his share of dirt — but now he was invisible! Without a moment's hesitation Hiro strode up behind the bully and pulled him off the smaller boy by his ears. Taro was surprised and tumbled to the ground, but he recovered quickly. He rolled over to face his attacker and — there was only empty air.

The words "What's going on here?" had just left the bully's mouth when someone or something stepped on his fingers. He screamed in fright and stood up. The younger boy spat out a mouthful of dirt and turned to see what was happening.

Confused and somewhat frightened, Taro blamed the smaller boy, and rose to kick him. "Why you . . . How did you do that?"

Hiro reached Taro before he could get to the smaller boy, and kicked the bully in the shins. Taro grabbed his leg in pain, balancing on one leg. The sight was too much for Hiro to refuse, and he gave the bully a shove that toppled him into a rice paddy by the side of the road.

The smaller boy brushed off his clothes and

ran home while Hiro, hands on his hips, laughed at the terror of the neighborhood. He was just a scared boy wallowing around in a muddy rice paddy now — thanks to the tengu and the coat of invisibility.

In a similar adventure, Hiro amused himself by playing the village's two smithies against each other. Wearing the coat, he stood in the middle of the street that separated the rivals and yelled, "Of course, I am the best smithy in all these parts."

Each brawny metal-worker heard what he assumed was the other boasting of his skills, and each gathered his apprentices and rushed into the street to take up the challenge.

"You're the best smithy?" asked the first blacksmith. "How can you say you're the best smithy in these parts when you can't even make a decent nail? You've got some nerve, amateur."

"I've never bragged about it," answered the second. "There's never been any need to — my work is obviously of a much finer quality than some rookie's crude slag."

Fortunately, some villagers separated the two before they came to blows. Grudgingly, the two started back to their furnaces. But Hiro was not satisfied with his mischief for the day.

While the street was full of people, Hiro walked between rival apprentices and delivered a blow aimed at the apprentices: "Only a second-rate apprentice would work for a second-rate master like yours."

The rival apprentices needed no further invitation and were upon each other in an instant. The villagers restraining the two smithies freed the men to separate the two apprentices, but as soon as they had done this, the two smithies began battling it out. The villagers, caught in the middle, became involved in the melee until the street was full of people punching, biting, poking and scratching each other. At this moment, Hiro took his leave and watched the battle from afar.

Another adventure began with a trip to the sweet store. Once Hiro had exhausted the mountain of sweets the tengu had thrown at him, he wanted more. Wearing the coat of invisibility, hiro paid a call on the sweet shop.

The owner of the shop was with a customer when Hiro snuck in. In the midst of exchanging the latest rumors from throughout the town, the owner suddenly spied a pastry filled with sweet bean-paste float into the air. It hung there for a moment before half of it disappeared into thin air. The owner said not a word, but pointed at the remaining half of the pastry, still floating in the air. His customer turned to see the pastry and ran out of the store, yelling about hungry ghosts and evil spirits.

The owner watched as the last half of the pastry disappeared. For a moment, all was quiet. Then a rice cake rose up and hung in the air before it, too, disappeared. The owner's eyes grew wide with fright as one by one his finest cakes and cookies suddenly floated up into the air and disappeared. This was all the owner could see, but, of course, the sweets all disappeared into Hiro's mouth.

The owner of the candy shop followed his customer's example and fled his store, where cookies continued to float up and away until Hiro had eaten his fill.

The owner of the candy shop called the merchants of the town together to tell them what he had seen. At the meeting, he discovered that several of his fellow shopkeepers had witnessed similar events. From the butcher's, choice meats had risen up and vanished, seemingly of their own volition.

The rice-broker found that someone had switched all the labels on his rice, so he mistakenly sent inferior, low-grade rice to the local daimyo, while villagers bought the best quality rice at the price of the lowest. Although the rice-broker found many new friends in the village, the daimyo was most displeased and threatened to have him arrested.

Perhaps the most frequently plagued merchant was the greengrocer, who was forced to take cover from tomatoes and melons that suddenly rose up and threw themselves at people.

Something was happening in the village, but no one was sure what was causing all the strange events.

One morning when Hiro was out with his friends, his mother found the filthy, tattered old coat in his closet.

"Where did this come from?" she wondered. "Hiro's been trading clothes with his friends again, I suppose." Without a second thought, she burned the dirty old coat with the trash.

Hiro came home and, upon finding the coat missing from his closet, asked his mother what had happened to it.

"Where did you get such a thing?" she asked him. "It was nasty, just nasty, so I burned it with the trash."

Hiro was shocked — his greatest treasure was no more. Slowly, he walked back to his room, wondering what to do next. The thought of finding another tengu crossed his mind briefly, but another thought soon crowded it out: the ashes!

He ran to the kitchen and asked his mother where the ashes of the coat were.

"Where do you think they'd be? In the ash pit in the back yard, naturally."

Hiro ran to the ash pit, where he stripped off all his clothes and began rubbing the ashes all over himself. Then he ran back into the house. He found his mother in the kitchen.

Quietly, Hiro lifted a knife from the table and held it before him. If his mother could see him, she would merely ask him why he was playing with the knife. If the ashes made him as invisible as the coat, she would be surprised to see only the knife floating in mid-air.

Hiro's mother looked up from the table. Out of the corner of she had seen the knife rise from the table. Now it was floating there, as though the spirits had come to claim her for their own. They were only waiting for the right moment to strike.

Hiro's mother screamed and fainted. Hiro ran back to the village market with a wry smile on his face. The ashes worked as well as the coat!

After a few hours of sweets, flying vegetables and other mischief, Hiro visited the booth of he village's *sake* maker. There he helped himself to a salty-sour *umeboshi*. The salty taste in his mouth left him very thirsty, so he grabbed a huge bottle of *sake* and drank mouthful after mouthful of the liquor, splashing *sake* all around his mouth.

The *sake* brewer, who was watching from behind the counter as his bottles emptied themselves, was startled to see first a pair of lips, then a mouth appear around the bottle. When the bottled floated back to its place on the counter, the mouth remained visible, hanging there in the air.

"Hey!" yelled the brewer, rising from his hiding place. "I'll get you for this!"

He took up a pole from behind the counter and started for the mouth. Hiro, thinking he was completely invisible, stepped aside to let the brewer pass out of the shop into the street. But the brewer raised his pole and, aiming just below the floating mouth, thwacked Hiro across the shoulders.

"Yaiiii!" shrieked Hiro, and he ran out into the street.

The brewer followed, yelling, "It's here! Whatever the thing is, it's here!" That was all the explanation necessary to send the other villagers into the streets. They understood the meaning behind the brewer's cries. "It's a mouth! It's a floating mouth!"

The villagers gathered quickly, and chased the mouth through the village.

Hiro ran as fast as he could, but the villagers stayed close behind. As he ran, Hiro's perspiration began to wash the ash away from his body, leaving part of his chest, a leg and the left shoulder visible to his pursuers.

The chase continued until both Hiro and the villagers slowed to catch their breath. The villagers now knew they were chasing an odd assortment of body parts, but Hiro had no idea how he had been discovered.

Finally, Hiro collapsed from exhaustion. The crowd caught up with him and began beating him with their poles and sticks. Their vengeance was merciless, and had they continued Hiro certainly would have been killed. Fortunately, a sudden spring storm sent forth a torrent of rain from the skies, washing the ash of invis-

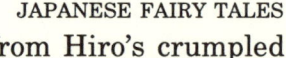

ibility from Hiro's crumpled body.

Despite the beating, the villagers recognized Hiro. But the discovery that their tormentor was one of their own did little to evoke feelings of pity among them.

Rejoicing, the villagers paraded back to the town, leaving Hiro, battered to within an inch of his life, to crawl home on his own.

Tsuru no Ongaeshi — The Gift of the Crane

A LONG time ago a very old, kind and gentle couple lived in the mountains of Japan. The man made his hard living as a woodsman, gathering bundles of wood and grass from the mountains and selling them to people in nearby villages. His wife added to the family's meager income by selling cloth she wove on a loom in their home.

One winter's day while the man was on his way home from another day of gathering wood, he passed by a swamp. The swamp, frozen over with ice, sparkled beautifully in the sunlight, and the man stopped to admire its beauty — and to catch his breath before continuing home with his heavy load of wood.

As he looked on the shimmering surface of the swamp, he heard the cry of a crane. It was not the usual confident cry of the majestic bird. The cry was mournful, dark with despair and pain.

Intrigued by the sad cry, the man looked closely to find the source of the crying. Leaving his load by the trail, he carefully made his way out onto the ice. The surface was solid, and the man was not worried about falling through the ice, but he did worry he might hurt himself. "If I slip and break my hip," he thought, "I'll die here. No one will find me until it's too late."

But the pained cry of the crane was too much to ignore, and the man continued across the frozen swamp to see what he could do to help.

Rounding a clump of frozen brush, he found the crane and knew at once why its cry was so sad. One of its legs had become pinned between two large blocks of ice. The crane was trapped on the swamp, and unless the old man helped free its leg, it would probably die there or fall prey to a hungry wolf.

The man didn't need to think twice about what was to be done. He set about freeing the crane's leg from the ice at once, and the task was completed swiftly.

Once the crane's leg was free, the bird stood and gave the man a look that can only be described as the happiest look a crane could give. then the great bird spread its wings and took to the sky. With a warm "Koooo, kooooo," the crane disappeared in the distance.

Pleased with himself, the man carefully made his way back to the path, where he picked up his bundle of wood and continued on his way home.

That night, the old man told his wife the tale of the crane.

"A crane?" she asked in surprise, "How beautiful. Such a nice thing you did." A warm smile spread across her face as she reassured herself her husband was the kindest man in the world.

The smile was fresh on her face as a she heard the *ton-ton-ton* of someone knocking on the old couple's door.

"Who could that be?" the woman wondered aloud. "So late at night and with so much snow?"

The old man also thought it strange to have a visitor so late a night, but he went to answer the door nevertheless. Ice and snow had piled up against the door and the man opened it with some difficulty. When at last he had managed to open the door, he saw standing before him the most beautiful young girl he had ever seen.

"Good evening," the girl said. "I seem to have lost my way in the darkness and the snowstorm. Could I impose on you and stay the night here tonight?"

The man was surprised and could not speak, but his

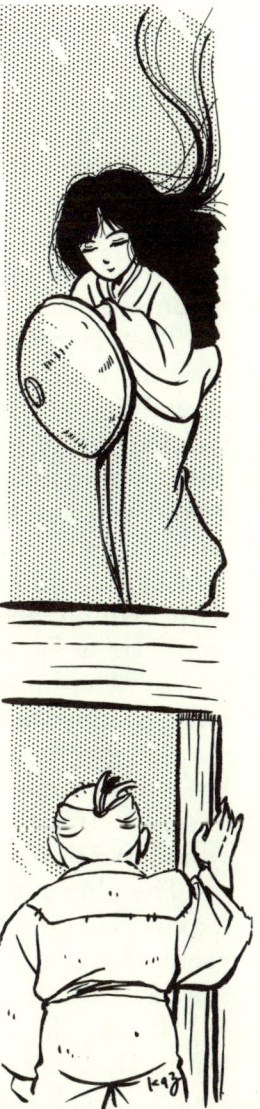

wife was soon by his side. "Certainly, my dear," she answered. "Please, come in and warm yourself by the fire."

The old couple prepared a meal for their guest. Meager though their fare was, they gave the girl the best portions of all the food. The two were overjoyed to have a guest, for they only very rarely did visitors pass through their part of the mountains.

They enjoyed talking with their guest, and over the course of their discussion, the girl revealed that she was headed to no destination in particular. At this, the old man looked at his wife, who nodded, and asked the girl, "What would you say to staying with us for a longer while?"

"You could be our daughter," said the old man. "Well, I mean, we have no children, and we would treat you as our own. I mean, er, that is to say..." The husband stumbled over his words, but his smile was honest and pure.

The girl answered with a smile as bright as the winter sun on a field on freshly fallen snow. "Yes. . . . If I would be no trouble for you, yes. I would like to stay here."

The old couple went to sleep in their room, leaving the girl to sleep in the warm common room. Warm under the covers, they thought of the day's events.

"It was the good turn you did freeing that crane that brought us such a lovely guest," spoke the old woman. "I hope she can stay with

TSURU NO ONGAESHI

us for a long time to come."

The woman did not put her feelings into words for she knew her husband felt the same joy: "We have been granted a child. At last, we have a child."

The girl awoke well before dawn to surprise her new family by preparing a fine breakfast for them. Undaunted by the darkness, she made her way to the small kitchen and looked about for food and pots. However, the girl soon discovered there was no food to be found. No miso for miso soup, no fish to grill, and not even a single grain of rice.

"What am I to do?" the girl asked herself. "I wanted to make life easier for the old couple."

Then, spying a spindle for spinning thread, her eyes brightened. The girl took the spindle and wandered about the old couple's tiny home until she found the room she was looking for — the room with the loom.

She slid the old door shut as quietly as possible and set to work. Soon the faint *ka-klackety-klack, ka-klackety-klack* of the loom echoed through the house.

The old couple awoke just before sunrise. When they found the common room empty they looked at each other in surprise — had their guest from the previous night been nothing more than a dream?

"The girl . . . where did she do?" asked the

man. His wife could only reply with a shrug of her shoulders.

The woman was on the verge of tears, but just before the first teardrops spilled out the girl came into the common room.

"*Ohayo gozaimasu*, good morning," she said to the startled couple. "I'm sorry if I made too much noise. Would you have a look at this?"

The girl raised her hands, in which the woman saw a section of the most beautiful cloth she had seen in her life.

The woman was speechless for a moment. Recovering, she said "It's marvelous. It's, it's very special . . ."

Her husband, who had seen enough of his wife's work to tell good cloth from bad, was equally impressed. "It . . . shines. It's so, so magical."

The old man and woman took turns looking at the cloth and holding it up to the faint sunlight to get a better look. It was truly marvelous work.

Pleased with the couple's response, the girl sat down and said, "Please sell it in the village. Use the money to buy rice and miso and other things you need."

As soon as dawn had broken, the old man went straight to the village to sell the marvelous cloth. Many in the town were interested in the cloth, and prospective buyers began offering the man money and goods until the man finally sold it to the highest bidder for a hefty sum. With the money from the cloth, he bought rice, miso and fish. As a gift for the girl, he bought a black lacquered comb to decorate her hair.

That night, the three had their first full meal — rice, miso, fish and other dishes — in what seemed like ages. The girl was delighted with the comb, and more delighted to see the happiness reflected in the faces of her "parents." The parents, in turn, were happy because their "daughter" was happy.

Just before bed, the girl retired to the weaving room, saying she would begin a new cloth for the next day. Before she left, she told the old couple she had but one thing to ask of them. With a solemn look on her face, she said, "I must ask you never to enter the weaving room while I am working there. Promise me you won't even look in the room while I am there."

"Of course," replied the couple. "Anything you say. We promise."

With that, the girl went off to work and the couple retired to their room. Their sleep was so filled with happy dreams that they never heard the soft *ka-klackety-klack, ka-klackety-klack* of the loom as the girl worked into the wee hours.

The next day the girl presented the man with a sheet of fine cloth, which he again sold in the town. The next day was the same, as was the next and the next. The girl had kept up her routine of weaving through the night for a week when the man began to worry about her.

"She never rests," he told his wife. "She's always doing something for us. Working, cleaning, weaving."

The woman was aware of what was happening. "She looks so tired, the poor thing."

That night, as the old couple prepared to sleep, the woman noticed a change in the sound of the loom. *Ka-klack-klack-klackety, ka-klack-klack-klackety* it went.

"Something is wrong," she told her husband. "That's not the way it should sound. Won't you go have a look at her? Make sure she's alright."

"Yes," the man agreed. "She's been pushing herself so hard these past few days."

The man stood and walked to the weaving room. As he approached the door, however, he remembered his promise. "But I gave my word never to look in the weaving room while she was working."

Suddenly, the sound of the loom stopped altogether.

The sudden change alarmed the man. In his mind's eye he saw his overworked "daughter" collapsed from exhaustion, slumped over the loom. He opened the door to the weaving room enough to look inside and check on the girl.

Instead of finding the girl working the loom, he saw a single white crane. The crane was plucking feathers from its own plumage and

weaving them to make the fine cloth. The crane winced in pain with each feather it tore from its breast. But it continued to pluck feathers, one by one, and weaving them into the fine cloth.

His jaw slack with disbelief, the man unthinkingly pushed the door open. The crane turned its head and, understanding the man had seen what was going on, drooped its head.

Slowly, the crane changed its shape back into that of the beautiful young girl.

"You're . . . you're . . ."

The old woman appeared by her husband's side.

"Yes," said the girl. "I am the crane you saved from the frozen swamp."

"The crane," the man said to his wife. "She's the . . . "

"Yes. We can change into human form just once. I owed you my life, and I sought to repay that debt as your daughter.

"But now that you have seen my true form, I can only retain my human for a few moments."

The woman began crying, and her husband soon joined him. The girl did not cry, though her face was a portrait of sadness.

"I am sorry things were not better for us," she said. "I must leave you now. Please remember me fondly, for I shall never forget you."

With that, the girl opened the window of the weaving room. The sky was dark, and a light snow was falling over the countryside. Silently, the girl changed back into a crane.

"Koooooo," the crane said sadly. The air shook as the crane's great wings flapped and the great bird rose slowly into the winter air.

On the floor the man saw the lacquered comb he had given the girl. He picked it up and called to the crane, "Something to remember us by." The crane turned and swooped down towards the old couple's home, whereupon the man tossed the comb into the sky. The crane caught the comb at the top of its arc. It slowly circled the couple's home once more, then disappeared into the winter sky with the comb in its beak.

Sadly, the old couple went back to sleep.

In the remaining years of their lives, the old man and his wife never failed to look when they heard the "kooooo, kooooo" of a crane making its way across the sky. With a tear of remembrance, they always watched the great bird slowly cross the sky and fade into the horizon.

Ubasuteyama —
The Mountain of Exile for the Elderly

Long ago there was a powerful kingdom called Satsuma in part of what is now known as the island of Kyushu. Among other things, the Satsuma kingdom was known for its great military strength. But it was also known for one peculiar law that concerned its older citizens. The rulers of Satsuma decided that old people were unproductive, and had little to contribute to what was then a growing kingdom. The leaders also concluded that old people were an unnecessary drain on the kingdom's resources. Therefore, they reasoned, to make better use of their limited resources, everyone sixty years old or older had to leave Satsuma. Those that refused to leave were killed, and severe penalties would befall any family caught sheltering anyone over the age limit.

Naturally, this law did not sit well with the people of Satsuma, who for many years had been taught to venerate their elders and treat them with the greatest respect. The laws of the land, however, were enforced with the greatest strictness, and over time the practice of sending old people away or abandoning them became expected, if not accepted.

Against this background there lived a woodcutter in a small village wedged between green mountains and a sparkling blue sea. Gompei, as he was called, was one citizen of Satsuma determined that his mother would not be killed or abandoned when she reached her sixtieth birthday. However, the only plan he could think of was to carry his mother deep into the mountains. There, Gompei thought, she could live the rest of her life safe from the Satsuma authorities.

Gompei cried as he told his mother of his plan. His mother was a gentle, wise woman, and she understood the pain Gompei felt in making his decision. She was more worried about the risk her son was taking in circumventing the law than for her own safety, but she agreed that his idea was their only alternative.

Early the next morning Gompei loaded his mother onto his back and, taking a blanket and a bag of food, set out for the mountains. After a few hours of climbing along a well-traveled path, Gompei turned off the trail and made his way through virgin forest.

Gompei stumbled occasionally as he climbed. The brush was thick and Gompei lost his bearings more than once as he continued up the mountain. Gompei's mother was silent her son carried her along, but Gompei could feel the moisture of her tears as they fell on his back.

Every so often the old woman reached out and broke branches from trees and bushes along the way. At first, Gompei thought she was trying to hold on to the trees, trying to resist what he saw as her inevitable exile to the top of the mountain. But after a while he realized this was not the case.

"Could you stop that, mother?" he asked "If I lose my balance and fall, we could both be hurt."

"I'm sorry, my son," replied the old woman. However, she did not stop grabbing and breaking branches every so often.

Finally, Gompei reached the top of the mountain. He set his mother down and spread out the blanket for her to sit on. The view from the top of the mountain was breathtaking. Like the sky, the sea was a bright, shimmering blue, and the different hues of green that carpeted the mountain were so beautiful Gompei momentarily forgot why he had climbed the mountain in the first place.

"This isn't such a bad place," said the old woman, reminding Gompei why he was there. "The view is very nice and there seem to be enough berries and other food for me to live on. You won't need to worry about visiting me every day."

Gompei looked at his mother and began crying once again. He had carried her into exile on the top of a mountain, turning her out to pasture as a farmer might an animal that had outlived its prime. Yet she was trying to ease his conscience and convince him she would enjoy her new home in isolation.

His conscience weighing down upon him, Gompei began making his way down the mountain to return to the village. Before he was out of earshot, his mother called to him. "You shouldn't have as much trouble getting home as you did getting up here. Just follow the path of the torn branches."

Gompei's heart grew heavier when he heard this. All the while he was climbing the mountain with his mother on his back, she was worrying about how he was going to get home! Gompei began to cry again. He thanked his mother, then turned to go back to his village.

Because his mother had made the path easy to follow, Gompei had no trouble finding his way back to the main trail, then back to his village. It was late in the afternoon when he finally arrived at his door. He was very tired, and he rolled out his sleeping mat at once. He thought he would fall asleep the moment his head touched the mat, but as soon as he closed his eyes he saw his mother, all alone on the mountain.

"Was she cold?" he worried. "What if a wolf came along? How would she defend herself? If it gets too cold, she will get sick, won't she — and it will be my fault, because I left here there, on the top of the mountain. I left my own mother alone in the wilds to die!"

His brain pounding, Gompei rose and left his home. Slowly making his way up the dark mountain path, he climbed to the top of the mountain to the spot where he left his mother.

"Mother?" he whispered. "Are you here? It's your son, Gompei. Are you here?"

He whispered loudly in this manner for a long time, circling the top of the mountain in search of his mother until finally he heard her whispered reply. "Here, my son. I am here."

Gompei followed the voice until he found his mother. He embraced her, and both began to cry.

"I am sorry, Mother. I will never leave you alone like this again. I promise. Return with me. I will hide you from the authorities, and you will be safe for the rest of your life."

Gompei's mother worried about her son's plan. If she were discovered, she might be killed on the spot. Dire consequences would most certainly befall Gompei and his family as well. But Gompei was determined not to leave his mother again. He had her climb on his back, and carefully felt his way down the mountain.

In the days that followed Gompei was very careful not to arouse suspicion regarding his mother. When he spoke with his neighbors he lamented that he had unwillingly but dutifully followed Satsuma law and sent his mother into exile. He cried tears at rage for the loss of his mother, and his neighbors sympathized with him, knowing that when the time came they too would be forced to exile their elders.

But at night, Gompei crept to a storage shed behind his house with a basket of food in his hands. He whispered the latest news and gossip to her, and told her how his family — her grandchildren — were growing up.

The lords of Satsuma, the men who made the proclamation that older people like Gompei's mother were to be banished, were perplexed. A messenger had come from a nearby kingdom bearing a challenge. If the lords of Satsuma did not accept the challenge, it would be a grave insult to the rulers of the nearby kingdom, and they would probably invade Satsuma. If they accepted the challenge, then failed to meet their rival's test, the nearby kingdom might view this as a provocation and take the opportunity to invade Satsuma.

Satsuma was a very strong kingdom, but the kingdom that sent the challenge was even stronger. Satsuma could defend itself in the short run, but the rival kingdom would certainly win any lengthy confrontation. Reluctantly, the great men of Satsuma accepted the challenge and called for the messenger.

"Great lords of Satsuma," began the messenger. "My general challenges you with tasks he hopes you will not view as too simple or too easy. Surely, a kingdom with resources as great as Satsuma will have little trouble with such challenges, but my general is interested in these issues as a matter of habit. Please show your respect enough by undertaking to present my master with a rope of ashes. You have one week to deliver the item so humbly requested." His message delivered, the messenger departed.

The lords of Satsuma were left scratching their chins. What was a rope of ashes, and how were they to get one? If they could not find a rope of ashes they were doomed. The general would send his troops, besiege Satsuma and claim the land for his own.

"Is there no one in the land who knows how to fashion a rope from ashes?" asked the Satsuma leaders. Instantly, their messengers set out across the kingdom, posting notices and making announcements asking anyone with any idea how to make a rope of ashes to come forth.

Naturally, these messengers came to Gompei's village, and Gompei included the news in his secret talks with his mother.

"A rope of ashes? Why would the great rulers of Satsuma want something so easily made? Here, let me tell you how to do it. Rub salt into a rope — any old rope will do, but make sure the salt is rubbed all through it. Then burn the rope. The rope will burn away, but the ashes will keep the ropes form. It's simple."

Gompei followed his mother's instructions and made a rope of ashes. He was surprised how easy it was to make. He sent the rope to the leaders of Satsuma, who rewarded him with a great bag of gold. Gompei took the gold and bought food and blankets for his mother. He used some of the money to strengthen the old shed where his mother was hiding, for the walls of the shed were not strong enough to keep out the winds of the coming winter.

The Satsuma leaders sent the rope to the rival general, who was surprised and disappointed. Nevertheless, he agreed they had met the challenge and produced a rope of ashes.

After a few weeks the rival kingdom sent another messenger to Satsuma. This time the challenge was a more obvious threat.

The messenger showed the assembled lords of Satsuma a ball. "My lord and master challenges you to pass one thread through the holes in this ball. If you fail, he will assemble his army and crush you, taking Satsuma for his own."

The lords of Satsuma looked at the ball. It had two holes in it, yet the holes seemed to curve and twist all through the ball, making it extremely difficult for anyone to pass a thread through it.

The Satsuma leaders tried their best, then they had their retainers try their best. When they all had failed, they again sent their messengers throughout the land to ask if anyone knew how to thread the mysterious orb.

As before, Gompei learned of the challenge before the leaders of his kingdom, and he told his mother about the mysterious ball.

The next morning Gompei appeared at the castle of the Satsuma lords and asked to be allowed to try to solve the challenge. Having solved the earlier puzzle, the lords welcomed Gompei with respect, but they all secretly doubted he could meet the test.

Gompei took a small box from a pouch slung on his shoulder, from which he produced an ant. He tied a thread around the ant's head. Next, he daubed a little honey on one of the two holes of the ball, and placed the ant into the other. The ant, smelling the honey, crawled through the ball to the other end. When it emerged, Gompei untied the thread from the ant's head, rewarded the insect with another daub of honey, and held up the threaded ball to show the assembled leaders.

The men of Satsuma were impressed, and rewarded Gompei once more with a great bag of gold. Gompei took the gold and returned home, buying more food and blankets for his mother along the way.

The men who ruled Satsuma were not surprised when a messenger from their rival kingdom visited a third time. He brought a third and final challenge for Satsuma.

"My esteemed leader's challenge to you, fine men of Satsuma," said the messenger, "is to construct a drum that will beat itself."

The men of Satsuma were very puzzled with this challenge, and attempted to question the messenger further, but the messenger would say no more. He rode off into the distance with the threat of invasion looming over the men of Satsuma once more.

This time the leaders of Satsuma did not waste time trying to solve the challenge themselves. They called immediately for Gompei, and presented the problem to him. Gompei accepted the challenge, and promised to have the drum that beat itself ready before the deadline.

The morning the messenger was due to return, Gompei walked to the castle and gave the lords of Satsuma a drum that did indeed sound itself. The messenger arrived in due time, and when he saw and heard the drum that sounded itself, he rushed back to his master to tell him the news.

"If they have truly constructed such a drum," said the rival general, "they must have a far greater wisdom than is to be found in my kingdom. It would be a foolish thing to challenge such wisdom again, for any land that can make a drum that sounds itself must surely be able to make weapons that can destroy my armies." The general immediately issued a sincere apology to the leaders of Satsuma.

The rulers of Satsuma assembled once more for a special celebration to thank Gompei for his service.

The greatest of the leaders made a great speech thanking Gompei for repeatedly saving the kingdom. Then, he asked Gompei to make a wish. He would, he said, grant anything that Gompei asked for.

Gompei did not hesitate to ask for the life of his mother.

"She is over sixty years of age, so according to the laws you have so graciously bestowed upon us she should have been sent into exile. However, I could not stand to part with my mother, so I have hidden her in a shed on my land. I ask you to spare her life, and allow her to live with me until her natural death. After all, it was she who told me how to solve each of the challenges."

The lord was angry momentarily, startled that anyone in his kingdom would dare to oppose one of his edicts. But remembering her great service, and that without the woman there would have been no kingdom for him to rule, he relented.

"But you must explain," he demanded of Gompei, "how did you construct the drum that sounded itself?"

Gompei asked for and was given a long spear, which he thrust into the skin of the drum. As Gompei jumped away from the drum, a cloud of bees swarmed from the drum out into the room, then out an adjacent window.

"I see," said the ruler of Satsuma. "You put

bees in the drum. The bees tried to escape, bouncing off the skin of the drum and making the drum sound itself. How clever."

He ruler stroked his chin in thought. After a few moments of silence, he spoke again. "Now, as for your mother. I decree she must be brought from your shed at once, where she may live a normal life until her natural death. Indeed, the wisdom she has accumulated — wisdom that may only be accumulated with time, mind you — has proven so valuable she and all others of her age *must* be allowed to live, to serve Satsuma with their wisdom and intelligence."

The regent began to speak excitedly. "In fact," he continued, "I hereby declare it a crime to mistreat older people, or to treat them with disrespect. Anyone breaking this law will be, will be killed — or at least exiled!"

Warashibe Chōja — A Fortune from Straw

The old man was angry with the world. A life of poverty and hardship had left him with a dark, pessimistic view of the world. Like so many other pessimists, rather than trying to make the best of his life, the old man did what he could to drag others down into his gloomy little world. One person around him who remained untouched by the old man's pessimism, despite poverty and hardships of his own, was the old man's son, Jun.

Jun was, in his father's eyes, a hopeless optimist. His father saw Jun's optimism as an unhealthy attitude toward life that would get the boy nowhere fast. The boy, however, was unmoved by his father's views. Seeing the world in its best light came naturally to the boy. When it was sunny, Jun was happy for the farmers who could work in the fields and the children who could go out and play and so on. When it rained, he was happy that the farmers would have good harvests because nature so generously supplied their fields with life-bringing water.

One influence behind Jun's rosy outlook on life was his name. The very character used for

Jun's name meant "profit" or "to get rich." His father never would have chosen such a bright, cheery name, but it was his wife's dying wish that the boy be named Jun, and the man honored her last request. Jun's mother died shortly after giving birth to him — another in the long list in Jun's father's list of injustices.

While Jun's father moaned about his poverty and the difficulties in life, Jun was happy that he and his father were together and in good health, and that they had a roof over their heads. In short, Jun always saw half a glass of water as one half full, while his father saw the same glass as half empty.

One afternoon, Jun and his father were working in the small field behind their home.

"Okay, Mister Optimist," called Jun's father from the far side of the field. "Here's one for you."

Jun knew his father was about to try to break down his optimism again with another of his trials. Jun enjoyed his father's attempts to break his faith. He thought of the banter between him and his father as a sincere, though misguided, expression of his father's love for him. He knew how hard his father worked, and he realized that his father was nothing short of unlucky. Jun's father worked twice as hard as his neighbors, but circumstances always seemed to work against him.

Jun, waiting for the challenge, turned to watch his father trooping across the field.

"Take this straw here and use it to make us

rich," said his father. "How's that? Can you handle that? Do you have the *optimism* to believe it will happen?" Jun's father made a sour face as he said "optimism," his least favorite word in the language.

"You never know until you try, do you?" answered young Jun. "I'm not sure how it can be done, but we'll never do it if we don't try, will we?"

Jun bundled the straw that had been lying in the field to dry. He tied the bundle with a strong rope, and he used the extra length of rope to tie the bundle around his shoulders. His father said nothing, but felt a twinge of remorse that his teasing might have hurt the boy.

"Have faith in me," said Jun, and he walked down the country road with the bundle of straw on his back.

"I have here a bundle of fine straw," cried Jun as he walked along the roads. "It was plucked from the earth by my father's own two hands. I'll sell it to you now for a thousand pieces of gold."

No one paid him and his offer any attention until he came to town. Jun took a spot in the town market and shouted his offer to all who would listen, and before long a crowd gathered around him.

"A thousand pieces of gold? For straw?" people asked. "What's so special about it? Is it magic straw or something?"

"No, just straw," replied Jun. "But my family is poor, and we need the money."

"So," asked an old man, "you want us to buy your straw — your normal, ordinary straw — for a thousand pieces of gold so you can become rich?"

"Yes."

The crowd laughed at Jun, and told him he was wasting his time. Why would anyone buy his straw when other people were selling straw for a fraction of Jun's price? Eventually the people went back to their shopping, leaving no one to listen to Jun shouting about his straw.

Word of Jun's sale got back to the other straw merchants, who met to discuss their new competition.

"That boy is no problem to us," said one of the merchants. "No one will ever buy his straw at the prices he's asking."

"That's the point!" bellowed a huge, muscle-bound

straw vendor. "He's making fun of us! Charging a fortune for his straw is his way of telling people *we're* charging too much for our straw!"

The other merchants agreed with the big, angry straw merchant, and they agreed Jun had to be stopped from selling his straw.

The five biggest, strongest straw merchants went to the spot where Jun was selling his straw. When they found Jun, he was making his sales pitch as enthusiastically as before, though no one seemed to be listening to him.

"Buy my straw!" he called. "I've got some fine straw here, just waiting to be made into thatch, or bedding for your animals. Straw here!"

"You're making a mockery of our business, boy!" roared the largest and scariest straw merchant. The others yelled at the boy and moved toward him menacingly.

Jun was an optimist, but optimism has its bounds. For a young boy to fight five huge, grown men was well beyond the bounds of optimism. Jun grabbed his straw and ran from the market as quickly as he could.

The five merchants were too big and slow to keep up with him, and Jun's escape was successful. Hanging his head in disappointment, he turned toward the road back to his home.

On his way back home Jun encountered a farmer at work in a field of *daikon*, great Japanese radishes. The *daikon* the farmer grew were known throughout the region as some of the largest, tastiest *daikon* around, and the farmer himself was a man well-respected in the land.

"Oh, this won't do," the farmer said half to himself as he stood looking at a pile of *daikon* he had gathered from his field. "This won't do at all. I *must* have something to tie these together."

Overhearing this, Jun asked the farmer if he could do with some straw.

"Why, yes," said the farmer. He took a bit of Jun's straw and tied it around a bundle of *daikon*. He took some more straw and tied it around another bunch of the great radishes, and before long he had used all the straw to bind his radishes into bundles.

Seeing he had used all Jun's straw, the farmer turned to him. "I used all your straw, and I would gladly pay you double what it is worth," he said, and Jun's face began to warm with joy. Fortune had smiled upon him, and he was going to turn the bundle of straw into a hill of gold in just one day.

"Unfortunately," continued the farmer, "all my money is at my house. I never carry any with me when I work. Would you take a bundle of *daikon* from me in exchange for your straw?"

Jun was disappointed, but a bundle of the man's famous *daikon* was much better than nothing at all, so he smiled and accepted the bundle.

Jun took the bundle of *daikon* and went back to the village market, where, taking care to keep well away from the straw merchants, he took a space and began advertising his goods.

"*Daikon* here! Famous, jumbo *daikon* here! Jumbo *daikon* for a thousand pieces of gold!"

Before long, however, word of Jun's return reached the straw merchants, and once more they chased him from the market. This time, however, Jun lost his way in the maze of roads leading through the town. The road he followed twisted and turned through several neighborhoods until Jun found himself in front the house of a very wealthy man.

The house was in great upheaval. Everywhere he looked, Jun saw servants and other people cleaning, moving furniture, cooking or doing laundry. Jun was intrigued, and went to the gate of the estate. There he asked one of the people working, a young girl, what all the commotion was about.

"My master, the wealthiest man in these parts, has passed away," she told him. "We are hurrying to make preparations for his wake. Soon relatives and others from all over will be here to mourn his passing."

No sooner had the girl begun her story than another servant called the girl in an angry voice. "You there. What are you doing standing there? Shouldn't you be working or something?" The other servant could not see Jun behind the gate, and only saw the idle servant girl.

"Yes, ma'am," replied the young girl. Then to Jun, she added. "That's Omari, the head cook here. She's just mad because the market is all out of *daikon* so the food for the wake is incomplete."

"*Daikon*?" asked Jun. "I happen to have something that might interest you."

Jun gave the girl the great bundle of *daikon*. With great difficulty, the girl took the bundle to the kitchen and showed the cook. The cook was overjoyed and apologized for yelling at the girl.

The girl then went back to the gate to talk to Jun. "Thank you! The cook was very happy. Thanks to your gift, the feast for the wake will be complete!"

The girl leaned over and kissed Jun lightly on his cheek. Then, she gave him a earthenware jar. "This is *sannen miso*. It's not much, but please take it in exchange for your *daikon*."

Jun, in a daze, blushed and accepted the jar of *miso*. Only after the girl had left did he remember how very precious *sannen miso* was. It was very rare, as it took years to ferment properly. *Sannen miso*, best known for its salty, bitter taste, was used to make a salty, bitter *miso* soup.

Jun danced along the road he though would lead him to his home. "One bundle of straw became a bundle of *daikon*," he thought happily, "and one bundle of *daikon* became a jar of *sannen miso*. Slow progress, but it *can* turn into a fortune!"

The road, however, did not lead to Jun's home. The sun was setting, and the skies grew darker and darker until Jun knew he had to find a place to sleep.

Jun stopped at the first farmhouse he found and knocked on the door. A blind old woman answered, and granted Jun's request.

"I am poor and have nothing to offer you. But if you will sleep on my floor you are welcome."

The woman welcomed Jun into her home, and Jun saw it was as she had said; there were only the most spartan furnishings, and only rice for supper. The woman offered him a bowl of rice, and Jun offered to use his *sannen miso* to make soup.

He made the soup quickly, and carefully handed a bowl to the woman. The woman took one sip of the soup and screamed at the top of her lungs. "WHHHHEEEEEEEEEEEYAAAAAAAA-AA!!!!" she screamed, hopping and jumping about the tiny home. "That's so SALTY!!!! And SOUR!!!!" she yelled, jumping so high she nearly reached to the ceiling.

Jun jumped to a corner of the tiny house to keep out of the woman's way. Then, when she had stopped jumping and regained her composure, she picked up the bowl again and looked at it.

"I can see!" she screamed with joy. "I can see again! That soup was so salty, so spicy . . ."

She stood and stepped into a back room, talking to Jun all the while.

"I am only a poor woman, as you can see," she said, her voice trailing off as she went from room to room. "Ah, here it is."

"Here," she continued as she came back to the room. "This is all I have. It is old and tired, but it is all I have to offer you. I am so happy! Now I can see my grandchildren."

The woman handed him a finely tooled katana sheathed in a colorful scabbard. It was a fine blade, and the little light in the old house reflected off the blade and made the room seem as bright as if it were daytime.

Happily, the old woman ran to visit her children's home, leaving Jun alone in the house.

She still had not returned when the sun rose the next morning, so Jun set out again without having a chance to thank her in person. He wandered along the road, wondering whether he was headed toward his home or away from it. As he wandered, Jun thought again how the bundle of straw had changed into a katana.

One bundle of straw into a bundle of daikon,
One bundle of daikon into sannen miso,
Sannen miso gives an old woman's sight back,
And sannen miso fetches this fine blade.
Things are going well for me.

Jun followed the road until it came to a great lake. The lake was a great highway for commerce, and trading ships crossed the lake a number of times each day. Jun asked the captain of a merchant vessel to take him to the other side.

"How much will you pay me?" the captain asked the boy.

"I have nothing for you now, but in time I will be a very wealthy man! Then I will pay you twice what the journey costs."

The captain laughed when Jun told him the story of how he had turned one bundle of straw into a katana, but he was impressed when he Jun showed him the great blade.

"This? The woman gave you this?" The captain was startled to see the blade. "Where did you meet this woman? Where did you get this?"

Jun told him more about the old woman as the captain listened eagerly. When Jun had finished his tale, the captain sat down in his chair, and looked off into space.

"I recognize this blade, boy. Long ago I was a warrior, and this was my leader's sword. This mark here," he said, pointing to a design on the scabbard, "is his family seal. If you have been given his blade, boy, you must surely be chosen for better things than this. The least I can do is help you across the lake."

With a smile, the captain welcomed Jun on board. He called his sailors together and immediately set sail for the far side of the great lake.

Jun sat on the deck, watching as the far shore grew closer and closer. The sun was bright, and Jun soon fell asleep in the warmth.

Soon, however, the sky grew dark. A fog began to rise from the lake, and Jun awoke with a foul air filling his lungs. Something was happening, and he rushed to find the captain to see what it was.

"We are lost, young master. These signs can only mean the great beast is upon us."

The words had scarcely left his mouth when the water before the ship began to bubble and seethe. Then a great dragon poked its head through the surface. It was an enormous beast.

Its head alone was nearly a third the length of the entire trading ship.

For a moment, the dragon only stared at the ship. Then, however, it moved toward the tiny vessel.

The captain found a spear and went to the bow of the ship. He staggered as the ship rocked on the waves, but climbed as close to the beast as he could. He waved the spear menacingly at the dragon, but the beast ignored him, taking in a great gulp of air, then unleashing a blast of breath so foul the captain lost his balance and fell back towards the main deck.

Jun leapt into action and unsheathed his great sword. He climbed the deck's railing and, taking a deep breath of clean air, jumped at the sea beast.

He landed on the beast's head and thrust the blade into his eye. The beast roared in pain and shook its head violently from side to side, but Jun held fast to the katana.

Quickly drawing the blade from one eye, Jun drove it as deep into the other eye as it would go. The dragon roared again, and shook more violently than before. Jun lost his grip on the katana and was thrown through the air as the beast thrashed about the lake. With a final roar of anger and pain, the dragon dove deep into the lake and disappeared.

The dragon had damaged the trading ship with tremendous waves, but the captain guided his vessel close enough to the boy for a rope to be thrown to him. The sailors hauled Jun on board, then began a lively celebration — the dragon had been defeated!

Jun's only disappointment was that he had lost his fine sword — he had left it in the sea dragon's eye.

When the crippled ship limped into port, the captain called all the captains of all the ships that sailed the lake and told them Jun had defeated the dragon, and that they need never fear the great beast again. Even if it survived, it was most likely blind — it would menace them no more.

The owner of the

captain's ship was delighted to hear of Jun's bravery in the defeat of the dragon. The dragon had sunk many of his ships, sending experienced crews — and shiploads of priceless cargo — to the depths of the lake. The owner was so happy to hear of the monster's defeat he gave Jun a reward.

He held a great feast for everyone in the town the very night the ship docked. At the height of the celebration he called Jun before him and told everyone assembled he was giving Jun his weight in gold. Jun sat in a scale the great merchant had ordered for the event, and the owner added gold coins to the empty arm of the scale until Jun rose in the air and the two arms balanced.

"This," said the merchant, "is your reward for saving my ship, its crew and its cargo. This is your reward for ridding the lake of the sea beast."

He turned to the crowd and cried, "One thousand pieces of gold!"

The crowd applauded and cheered.

"One thousand pieces of gold and the rank of honorary captain in my merchant fleet."

Jun thanked the great merchant and the captain and his crew. The celebration continued until the next morning, when Jun set sail for the far port again.

When he returned, he borrowed a horse and cart from the merchant's stables and set out for his home. He arrived home to find his father still at work in the field. When he showed his father the great fortune he had made from just one bundle of straw, all the old man could do was cry with happiness. For once, he didn't mind his son's great optimism.

Furuya no Mori —
The Wolf and the Horse Thief

Long ago, an old man and his wife lived in a village at the foot of a steep mountain range. They had very little money, so they made do with a house made of straw. The walls were very fragile, and the roof, of thatch, was on the verge of coll apsing whenever a heavy rainstorm struck.

One of the few respites the couple found from the harsh realities of their poverty was their horse. The old couple loved their horse so much that when times were especially bad they would rather go hungry than make their horse do without food.

In due course, this horse gave birth to a fine pony. Over time, the pony grew larger and caught the eye of a horse-trader that regularly travelled through the region.

The horse trader asked the couple if they would part with the fine young horse. The couple hesitated, but the trader was very interested in the pony. He offered the couple more money every time they refused until finally they could not refuse.

"But," the old woman said, "he is so young

now. If you come back in a month or so we will sell him to you at the price we agreed on."

The trader agreed to return in one month with the money to buy the pony, and happily went on his way.

Later, the old woman was shopping in the village market, where she told a neighbor of the good fortune that had come to her and her husband. Though she was sad to part with the pony, she was happy to think they would have enough money to pay some of their debts, maybe even enough money left over to repair or rebuild the house.

However, the old woman's neighbor was not the only person in the market listening to her story with intense interest. Another horse-trader passing through town overheard the story of the magnificent pony and the great price it would fetch in only a month's time.

As he heard the woman's tale the second horse-trader became consumed with the desire to have the old couple's horse for himself, thus improving his stock of horses to his rival's loss. But this horse-trader was nowhere near as honest as the first trader. Rather than approach the couple and try to outbid his competitor, the second trader planned to follow the old woman home and steal the horse under cover of darkness.

The woman returned to her straw home in the early afternoon, with the dishonest horse-trader following behind her at a safe distance. He stopped at a hill just before the old couple's home, where he decided to wait for nightfall.

After a while it began to rain. It began with a light shower, so the trader pulled his collar up and decided to wait under some trees nearby. But the rain and wind gathered intensity until it became clear to the trader that he was outside in the middle of one of the greatest storms in years.

He sneezed, and cursed his luck at having to be out in such a downpour, but his spirits rose when he thought of the fine pony that was his for the taking. Besides, he thought, it would be harder for him to be detected in the wind and rain of such a great storm. Cold and tired, the trader fell asleep in the rain.

At about the same time the dishonest horse-trader was catching cold, a huge wolf stirred in his den in the mountains above the village.

"I'm hungry," thought the wolf. "I'm so hungry I could eat a — a horse! That sounds good! There won't be anything to hunt in the woods tonight with this storm, but I'm sure the animals in the village will be tied up and unattended. It'll be easy. Somewhere down there I'll find a horse that's just right for the taking."

The great wolf went down the winding trail to the village and stopped to look over the first farmhouse he found. It was a small farmhouse, but it was well supplied with chickens and ducks. But the wolf was looking for a horse, and there would be no satisfaction in his belly until he found what he was after.

After two more farmhouses without horses, the wolf finally stumbled on a poor house made almost entirely from straw. Circling it, he found a shed in back of the house, and in the shed, he spied a horse and a fine young pony.

The wolf kept circling the farm, finally deciding that the best way to approach the shed without waking the animals and having them alert the humans to his presence was to go use the path from the house to the shed.

As the wolf started toward the house, the dishonest horse-trader began to make his way over the hill to the horse shed. The noise of the storm, he was sure, would conceal any noises the horses might make. "What luck," he thought, "to have stumbled onto a horse such as this. And it's all so easy!"

The noise of the storm deprived the old couple of one of their few free pleasures, their sleep. After tossing and turning, the two finally gave up trying to sleep altogether and began talking.

The wolf, passing by the house at this time, heard the old woman ask her husband, "What is the one thing you are afraid of more than any other?"

The wolf stopped and listened. It wasn't often he could eavesdrop on humans. He strained his ears against the rain.

"More than anything else, I'm really afraid of . . ."

A flash of lightening and a clap of thunder sent the wolf scampering away from the straw house before he could hear the old man's reply. Angry with himself for allowing a little thunder to frighten him, the wolf quickly crept back to hear the rest of the old couple's conversation.

". . . it could come down on us anywhere, at any moment, especially on a night like this. There would be nothing we could do about it. It would be awful. I only hope we aren't around it when it drops."

Crouched against the straw wall, the wolf wondered what it was that frightened the old man so. Within his breast he was disappointed that the old man wasn't frightened to death by wolves, but his curiosity outweighed his disappointment. What was the man — and by extension, the wolf mused, all men — afraid of more than anything else? It wasn't any natural calamity he knew of, nor did it sound like any animal he had ever encountered.

Whatever it was, thought the wolf, it dropped on its victims from above, and once it struck there would be nothing the victim could do to avert its fate. And they said it was likely to strike tonight? The wolf's curiosity was slowly replaced by apprehension, then fear. What was this thing, this thing humans found more frightening than a wolf? What if it struck tonight? Was it likely to attack a wolf?

The wolf's belly rumbled with hunger, pushing thoughts of fear far from his mind. He left the straw house and approached the shed.

The same clap of thunder that sent the wolf scrambling away from the farmhouse woke the horse-trader from a shallow, feverish sleep. Springing into action, he crept over the hill to the shed behind the straw house. Slowly, cautiously, he looked around the corner of the shed.

The wind had blown open the door of the shed, and from just outside the door the wolf could see the sleeping forms of the horse and her pony. But rather than slink in and attack his prey, the wolf hesitated uncharacteristically. The old man's words lingered in his mind, making him take extra precautions.

Still standing before the doorway, the wolf strained his eyes to penetrate the darkness of the shed. The forms of the two horses were clear, but the wolf was worried about the ceiling. Was the beast there, waiting for him? Was the beast that was especially likely to strike on a night like this night waiting for the wolf to enter and become his dinner?

The horse-trader looked around the corner of the shed. To his surprise, he saw a pony standing before the shed! It must have broken free in the storm! Wonderful! Now it would look like the pony had broken loose on its own and escaped into the night. No one would suspect theft! Such luck!

Seizing the opportunity, the trader leapt at the pony and landed squarely on its back. He quickly reached around the horse's neck and locked his arms tightly.

The wolf's heart pounded as he felt arms closing around his neck. "It's that thing!" the wolf thought.

"It's the creature the old man was so afraid of! It dropped down on me!"

The wolf jumped and squirmed to free himself from the creature's grasp, but the monster held tightly to his neck. The wolf tried to turn his head to look at his attacker, but the beast held his neck so firmly it was all the wolf could do to stay on his feet.

The wolf jumped and bucked with all its might, trying to throw the monster from its back. When this failed, the wolf began to run. He ran with all his might, turning and twisting at odd intervals to throw the monster off. Paying no mind to where he was going, the wolf ran as fast as he could towards the heart of the village.

"What a frisky little pony she is," thought the horse-trader as he held on to what he thought was a bucking young horse. "So healthy, so full of life! She'll bring a pretty penny when I sell her." Thinking of the profits he would have when he sold the pony, the trader tightened his grip.

The trader was a bit surprised that the pony continued to jump and buck when most horses would calm down after a short while. He was more surprised when the pony stopped jumping and began running toward town as fast it could.

"She's just frightened of the storm and all," he thought, and he vowed to hang on to his prize until it surrendered.

The wolf ran faster and faster, gaining speed

all the way to the village. The trader began to worry that the pony was going a bit too fast for his liking. He was afraid it was going too fast for him to jump off. But he discounted his fears with the thought that this was the mark of a truly fine pony — wild, strong and uncompromising. He strengthened his resolve to ride the pony until it was too tired to fight.

But he hoped the pony would give in soon. The first light of dawn was just beginning to creep over the hills.

The wolf continued racing toward the town at top speed. Whatever it was — the monster that dropped from nowhere and was more terrible, more frightening than anything else the old man had ever encountered — it was on his back. The terror gave him new energy in his flight.

The odd pair raced up a great hill just before reaching the town. Heading down the hill and into the town, the wolf gained speed. The storm had blown away and at this point the wolf and his rider were bathed in the first light of dawn. Thinking of his fortune, the man looked down at the pony to see his catch.

"Something's wrong here?" he thought, confused at the un-pony-like appearance of his mount. His mind was frozen with horror as he realized he was not riding a majestic young pony after all.

"WOOOOOLLLFFF!!!!!" he screamed at the top of his lungs. "WOOOOOLLLFFF!!!!!" But what could he do? Fear of the wolf paralyzed him, and the wolf's speed made jumping off unthinkable.

"Save me, preserve me, help me, somebody, something!" Panic-stricken thoughts raced through the wolf's mind. "It's riding me! It's trying to tire me out! It's just toying with me before it takes me to my doom."

Scarcely had these thoughts entered the wolf's mind than the monster on his back screamed a blood-chilling scream that made him run even faster down the hill.

More frightened than ever, the wolf began howling in fear. "AWOOOO-OOOO-OOO!!!!"

The first person to rise in the old village was the tofu maker, who woke well before dawn to prepare the day's tofu for sale. Having finished his morning chores, the tofu-maker was enjoying a moment to himself, taking in the sunrise.

Off in the distance the tofu-maker heard a most unusual noise. Normally, the only sounds he would hear at this hour would be his neighbors' chickens and the odd crow of a rooster. But this sound was different.

The man looked around the corner to the main road through the village to see what could be making such a racket. Off in the distance, the man saw an odd shape coming down the hill.

The wailing noise grew louder, and the tofu-maker heard his neighbors begin to stir as the noise woke them.

The tofu-maker watched the shape as it came closer and closer. Finally, the shape was close enough for him to see what it was — a wet, poorly dressed man riding a giant wolf, both the wolf and the rider screaming at the top of their lungs.

The tofu-maker was mesmerized by the sight, and stood rooted to the spot as the wolf and the horse-trader ran through the village, wailing all the while.

He watched as the rider and his strange mount rode out of the village, and he still had not moved when the two disappeared into the distance.

The wailing had roused several villagers

from slumber. "Tofu-maker," cried one. "What's all the screaming? What's happening?"

Not believing what he had seen, the tofu-maker rubbed his eyes before answered. "Nothing," he called back. "Nothing at all. You go on back to sleep. There's nothing going on here."

The old couple at the farm, having talked all night long, rose with the first rays of light. The old woman went to check on the animals while the old man walked about the farm looking for signs of damage the storm might have done. Finding none, the man began examining the roof and ceiling of their thatched home.

"The horses are just fine," the woman reported to her husband.

"The roof looks like it made it through well enough," he said, "but you never can be too sure. It could come down anywhere, at any moment, especially on a night like last night. I guess there's nothing we can do about it. I just hope we aren't around when it comes down."

The Racing Rice Cake of Fortune

Along, long time ago a poor couple lived deep in the mountains of Japan. The man worked as a woodsman. Every morning he awoke before dawn and set out for the hills, where he would cut wood and grass to sell in nearby villages. For lunch every day he would eat a ball of rice that his wife would prepare for him.

One afternoon, after a particularly hard day of cutting grass, the man sat down and took out his lunch.

"How lucky I am to have such a wonderful wife," he thought as he stared at the ball of rice, "who wakes up early to make my lunch for me." And though we're poor, she never complains about our lot in life. How lucky."

Warmed by these thoughts, he lifted the ball of rice to his mouth. But in the instant before he bit into the rice ball, it slipped from his grasp, tumbled to the ground and began to roll away. The man jumped up and grasped at the ball of rice, but it was just out of his reach.

The man chased the ball of rice, but it rolled down a mountain path as if it had a will of its own. It rolled just slightly faster than the man could run. When he slowed down to catch his breath, the ball of rice seemed to slow down as well. Rather than flee through the trees and underbrush, the ball followed the trail as it turned and twisted through the hills.

Finally, after what seemed like hours, the rice ball relented and allowed itself to be caught. The man happily retrieved his meal, but his joy was short-lived. He realized that the chase had taken him far from his fields. Indeed, he was far from any fields he recognized. He looked at the trail and it, too, was unlike any other he had crossed before. He had taken pride that in all his years in the hills he had never gotten lost; but now he knew he was completely, totally lost.

In despair, the old man sat down and ate his rice ball. Darkness fell quickly, and the man debated the merits of spending the night where he was versus trying to find his way home in the dark.

"Stay put," he thought. "It'll be morning again in a few hours and I can go home then. If I try to move now I'll probably twist my ankle or hurt myself."

But after a few more moments the man began to think of his wife.

"She'll be worried when I don't come home. She may stay up waiting for me to come home. She goes to such trouble to make my lunch for me. . . . Maybe I should go home . . . or at least try."

THE RACING RICE CAKE OF FORTUNE   71

The old man stood up and started wandering down a path the old man hoped led back to his village. Shortly, however, the man realized he had no idea where he was going. If he continued wandering around the forest, he might spend the whole night going in circles. At that moment it started to rain. Completely despondent, the old man sat down again.

As he sat down, however, a light caught his eye. "A light!" he said aloud. "There must be a house nearby! Maybe I can stay the night there."

The man hurried through the rain to find the house, but when he reached the light, he found nothing more than a weather-beaten old hut. "Any port in a storm," he thought with a chuckle, and slid open the door.

The first thing he noticed was that the inside of the hut was very, very bright. Next, he saw that the hut was much larger than it appeared from the outside. The ceiling was high, with a little loft built on the rafters. The only thing in the hut was a huge Buddhist statue made of stone.

Thinking he was alone, the man spoke aloud to the statue. *"Konban wa.* Good evening."

"Konban wa," replied the statue.

The man was startled, but strangely calm. With the sort of day he had been having a talking statue was just another oddity on a long list of oddities.

"Would you be so kind, please, as to allow me to pass the night here?"

The statue did not answer, so the man sat down on the floor and prepared to sleep. But as tired as the man was, the room was too bright for him to sleep. He stood up and looked around the room, but he could not find where the light was coming from.

"More magic," he thought. He sighed and resigned himself to trying to sleep in the brightness. But the brightness was such that no matter how he tried to sleep, no matter if he covered his eyes with his shirt, it was still to bright for him to sleep.

"Statue, I don't want to seem an ungrateful guest. But the light in this room is a bit extreme, wouldn't you say? Do you think you could turn it down a bit?"

"Come here!" the statue ordered. Surprised at the commanding tone of his voice, the man meekly walked up to the statue.

"Climb up on my knee," said the statue, and the man obeyed.

THE RACING RICE CAKE OF FORTUNE 73

"Climb up on my shoulder," said the statue, and the man climbed up to the statue's shoulder.

"Climb up onto my head," came the next command, and the man hesitatingly climbed up and balanced himself on the giant statue's head. The man was a little frightened — not of the statue, but because he was an old man, and his balance and reflexes were not what they had once been. The statue's head was a full eight feet off the floor. If the man lost his balance he would fall to the ground and injure himself for sure. Slowly, carefully, he balanced himself on the head of the statue and waited for the next command.

The statue seemed to wait a very long time before it gave the next command. "Climb up to the loft," it said, and the man obeyed.

On the floor of the tiny loft was a parasol made of paper and bamboo. The statue told the old man to quickly open and close the parasol so as to make as much noise as possible. Again, the man followed his instructions.

The next command befuddled the man even more than the others. "Continue making noises with the parasol," the man was told. "And crow like a rooster."

"Kokekokkoooo!" cried the man in his best imitation of a rooster. Over and over again, *"Kokekokkoooo! Kokekokkoooo!"*

After three or four minutes of playing with the parasol and crowing like a rooster, the statue told the man to stop. The man was short of breath, and complied readily.

"You may stay the night," said the statue, "but you must sleep in the loft and do exactly as I tell you." Having followed the statue's odd instructions thus far, the man agreed. Slowly, the room darkened, and the man fell fast asleep in the loft.

After a few hours of sleep, the man was startled to hear a great commotion below him. It was as boisterous and as merry as the village's harvest festival, but it was so loud it sounded as if several villages were holding their celebrations together.

The man rolled over to see what was happening below him, but before he looked down from the loft he heard the statue's voice again. "Close your eyes. Do not look at anything!"

Remembering his pledge to do exactly as the statue commanded, the man shut his eyes tightly.

The statue spoke again, "Pick up the parasol and act like a rooster again, exactly as you did before."

The man thought to open his eyes to find the parasol, but he decided against it, thinking that even an innocent violation of his agreement would be a violation nevertheless. Cautiously, he groped about the loft for the parasol. Finding it, he stood up and began shaking the parasol. Then he crowed as he had done earlier. *"Kokekok-koooo! Kokekokkoooo!"*

Over the sound of his parasol and crowing,

the man heard a deep, unearthly voice ask, "Is it dawn already? Quick! Let's go!" After the voice, the man heard what he could only assume was the sound of a great number of people running out of the hut in panic. The harvest celebration that he heard was put to an abrupt end.

After a few more moments, the parasol and his crowing were the only sounds to be heard. The man wondered if it would be safe for him to stop crowing like a rooster, since he was getting very tired. But he decided it would be worse to disobey the statue than to get a little tired, so he vowed to continue until the statue told him otherwise.

The statue was quick to stop him. "Stop and come down now."

The man climbed down from the loft to the head of the statue. Planting one unsure foot, then another on the statue's head, the man then balanced himself and hopped down to its shoulder, then its knee, then back to the floor.

As the man recovered some from his activity, the statue again spoke to him. "All this I give to you."

"What money?" asked the man. Turning around, he saw the floor of the room was strewn with gold, silver and precious gems.

"Th-, thank you," replied the man falteringly. He found among the treasure a great sack of strong material. Into this he placed all the treasure he could carry, and set out for home.

He eventually found his way home, where

his wife rushed to his side, thankful her husband was alive and well. She was even more overjoyed when he showed her the bag full of treasure.

Naturally, word of the woodsman's good fortune spread throughout the region. Not everyone was happy to hear of the woodsman treasure, for in every region of the world there are always those who, rather than rejoice upon hearing of another's happiness, only ask why they, too, did not have such good fortune.

One such person was a cranky old man living not too far from the woodsman's home. He was a most unremarkable man, save for his thoroughly sour disposition. He was rude to his neighbors, cruel to animals and he never returned things he borrowed from other people. He was not well liked in the region.

He had been the provincial tax assessor, but he lost his post when he backed the wrong side during a change of governments in the capital. Still, he lived well enough without having to work; he had stolen enough tax money during his time as an assessor to ensure a comfortable life, and he was miserly enough to make his small sum go a long way.

When the former official heard of the woodsman's good fortune, he decided to pay him a social call. The woodsman was immediately suspicious. Though he was a friendly person by nature, he knew the former official was not a nice man. He also knew that the greedy man would never visit anyone unless he had something to gain.

The miser was uncomfortable with people, especially now that he no longer held power as a tax assessor. He was most distressed to make small talk with the woodsman before coming to the point of his visit.

"I have heard of your great fortune, my friend," he told the woodsman.

The woodsman winced visibly at being called the miser's friend, but only nodded in reply.

"I trust you have reported your luck to the proper authorities?"

"That's no business of yours now, is it?" replied the woodsman. It was a stab at the miser's former glory.

The jab hit home as the miser lost his temper. "Of course it isn't, you fool!" yelled the miser. Then, recovering, "I mean, I only hope your newfound fortune doesn't cause you any trouble with the government. You know they can be so, so uncompromising."

"Yes, I remember well," said the woodsman dryly. "State your business and be on your way."

"It is simple — tell me how you found your fortune."

"It's no secret. You haven't heard it from someone else?"

"No, I want to hear it from you."

The woodsman relented. The hut where he had found the fortune was deep in the mountains, and he doubted the miser could find it no matter how he tried. He had nothing to lose by telling him the same tale he had already told the rest of the villagers, so he began in detail the tale of the animated rice-ball that led him to his fortune. Kind soul that he was, the woodsman told the miser the entire story of how he found his fortune. When he had finished, the miser thanked him and set out for home.

The next morning the miser rose and made himself a rice ball. Tucking it into his pouch, the miser set out for the mountains where the woodsman said he found his fortune.

The miser reached a clearing similar to the one where the woodsman first tried to eat his lunch. Expecting the rice ball to lead him to the treasure hut, he dropped the rice ball. However, rather than rolling away of its own accord as the woodsman's rice ball had done, the miser's rice ball landed with a thud and did not move.

The miser picked up the rice ball and

dropped it again, and again it did not move. Irritated, the miser kicked the rice ball. Rather than rolling, the rice ball broke into several small pieces, each of which and stay-ed where it fell. "*Chikushō*! You'll roll for him, but not for me, eh?" said the miser, getting angrier with each passing moment.

Finally, the miser had an idea. He took a ball from his pocket and carefully pressed the bits of rice around the ball so they would stick. Then, he dropped his "improved rice ball" to the ground. It only rolled a few feet before coming to rest next to an old pine tree, but the miser was undaunted. He kicked the new ball and followed it through the forest.

After less than an hour of kicking the rice ball and chasing after it, the man was too tired to go on. Being a miser, the man had little time for exercise or any other activity that did not increase his fortune measurably. Aside from lending money to his neighbors at usurious rates, his main activity was sitting around his home counting his money.

Still, the man persisted in kicking the rice ball every five minutes or so, then following it through the woods, wheezing and puffing all the way. Finally, night fell. According to the woodsman's story, he found the old hut with the statue in it shortly after dusk. "So," thought the miser, "all I have to do is wait until I see the light from the hut."

After straining his eyes for several hours, the miser grew frustrated. His eyes were tired and his head hurt. In despair, he talked to himself to get his spirits up. "It's got to be here! It *has* to be. Why would such fortune strike so randomly? It has to be here, waiting for me! Yes, waiting for me — so I should go after it, rather than wait for it to come to me! That's it!"

With that, the miser rose and began walking through the woods looking for the hut. The sky was black as coal, and the miser could not see the trail. He was scratched by thistles and briars which seemed to attack him with a will of their own, but he forgot his injuries when he saw a flickering light off in the distance.

He set out for the light at once. He could not tell how far away the light was, but he knew it couldn't be too far. Still, when he had not reached the light after half an hour of stumbling through the forest, he began to wonder. Was the light moving, shifting its position to tease him? He tried not to think about this possibility, concentrating instead on making his way through the forest. Unerringly, he managed to find every

THE RACING RICE CAKE OF FORTUNE 81

patch of poison ivy and every mosquito breeding-ground on the mountain. His most painful moment was when he walked straight into a pine tree. Clutching his nose in pain, the miser jumped back. The ground gave way beneath him, and he tumbled down a shallow ravine into a cold, cold stream.

Overriding all this, however, was the man's belief that somewhere in the dark, dark night there was a great heap of gold just waiting to be taken — by him, of course. This thought kept him going through all the pain and punishment the mountain dealt him.

Finally, the forest gave way to flat land leading up to the hut. The man raced to the hut, expecting to find the great pile of riches the woodsman had told him about. But all he saw was the great Buddhist statue of the woodsman's story.

Remembering what the woodsman's tale of what he had done, the miser rushed to the statue and without so much as a *"konban wa,"* climbed in turn on the statue's knee, shoulders and head. While trying to climb from the statue's head into the loft, the man lost his balance and slipped to the ground with a *thwump*. He landed on his wrist, adding a sprain to the great list of injuries he had suffered during this long night.

Deftly, he made his way back up to the statue's head, where he successfully made it to the loft. In the loft, the miser found the parasol the woodsman had mentioned. The miser picked it up and began opening it and closing it. Then he thought he remembered that the statue had told the woodsman to dance around, so he tried his best to dance — on his tired, battered legs — while he opened and shut the parasol with only one good hand.

The man remembered also that the woodsman had made rooster noises, so the miser began to do this as well. His voice cracked with pain as he did his best to *"kokekokkoooo!"* as a rooster would. Over and over again, *"Kokekokkoooo! Kokekokkoooo!"*

Exhausted from his long day, the man went to sleep on the floor. He only intended to sleep for an hour or two, but it seemed like many hours later when he was awakened by a great commotion on the ground floor of the hut. Shuffling feet and grumbling voices gave way to what sounded like a great feast. It sounded just like the woodsman had said it would, as if a whole village of people were having a great party, or holding market day on the little hut.

Singing voices tried to be heard

over other voices haggling about prices, while the cheers of lucky gamblers clashed with the sighs of those less fortunate. He was sorely tempted to look over the rail and see just what was going on below him, but he remembered the woodsman had told him he had promised the statue not to look. "Still," the miser thought, "the woodsman made the promise, not me. I could look. If I wanted to." But he thought the better of it.

The miser waited what he thought was an hour, then picked up the parasol. All at once, he began his dance, opening and closing the parasol as he called, *"Kokekokkoooo! Kokekokkoooo!"*

The party below him started to break up. Voices murmured and feet shuffled. It sounded as if crates were being loaded on a wagon — "Impossible," thought the miser. "How could anyone get a wagon in this tiny hut?"

"Dawn? Again?" a voice roared. "Time seems to skip right by when you're having fun, eh, boys?"

"When you're winning, you old fox," answered another. "The hours crawl by when you lose like I did tonight."

"Quick!" cried an harsh voice. "We don't have time to take it all. Let's go!"

The miser heard a crashing, metallic sound which his miserly ears readily identified as the sound of gold coins clinking against one another.

"Gold!" The miser's thoughts slipped from his mouth. He stopped making his rooster noises and dropped the parasol. The sound of gold drove all thoughts of caution from the miser's mind. Forgetting the woodsman's promise never to look down from the loft, the miser ran to the edge of the loft and looked. Sure enough, there was a great bag of gold on the floor. It looked as though it had been dropped by someone leaving in a hurry. Coins were scattered here and there, with diamonds and other precious gems mixed all about.

But the miser also saw two great demons on the floor below him. And they both saw him.

"Hey!" one demanded. "Who are you? What are you doing here?"

"A human?" roared the other. "Here?"

The man was paralyzed with fear, which was just as well. The only way out of the loft was to climb down the statue or to jump over the railing, either of which would leave him on the ground level with the waiting demons.

"Hey, everybody!" The first demon stomped on the floor and a trap door opened. The demon stuck his head in the doorway and bellowed, "Come back, everybody! It's not really dawn yet. We've been had."

"This *human* has made fools of us all!" yelled the second demon angrily. He began climbing the statue. The miser remained rooted to the spot.

One, then two, then three demons poked their heads through the trap door. They climbed out and were followed by two, then three more demons.

"Tricked?" asked a shaggy demon.

"He was up in the loft acting like a rooster, trying to make us think the sun was coming up."

"Hey, of all the dirty — I lost all my gold last night!" moaned a demon with his fur coated with layer upon layer of dirt and mud. "I thought the sun was coming up, and I was in such a hurry to get out of here I left everything!"

"So did I!" yelled another demon.

"Most of us did. Well, Mr. Human, we're going to teach you not to mess with demons. Get him."

Two demons grabbed the miser and tossed him from the loft into the waiting arms of the others below. They bit him and gnawed at him and tore the flesh from his skin, inflicting horrible torture after horrible torture upon him until the sun really was coming up.

"Well, we have to go now," said the dirtiest, nastiest demon (who had, coincidentally, lost the most money the previous night). "It's been fun, but now it's time to kill you."

The man dragged his bloodied body before the statue and pleaded for mercy. "Save me, statue," begged the man. "Just spare me my life."

The statue spoke to the miser for the first time. "Your greed has led to this. But I am merciful. Your life is spared."

The demons said nothing, but made frightening faces at the miser as they rushed to get through the trap door before the sun came up.

The greedy man was thankful that his life was spared, and bowed low before the statue. Then,

JAPANESE FAIRY TALES

slowly and with great effort, the miser began crawling home.

Shitakiri Suzume — The Tongueless Sparrow

The first rays of sunlight crept through the window and woke the old man. Quietly, so as not to disturb his sleeping wife, he crept to the kitchen, where he whispered, "Good morning! Good morning, friend!"

There was a fluttering noise, then a sparrow hopped up from the floor to the table.

"Good morning, father. Did you sleep well?" asked the sparrow.

"Indeed," replied the man. "I feel so rested I want to go to work *now*! But I think I'll wait until I have a little breakfast. What would you like?"

"I am not so hungry yet," chirped the sparrow.

The man made his breakfast and ate it as he watched the fat, red sun rise over the mountains. The sparrow perched beside him and watched silently. The man and the bird had been friends for many years, and they began almost every day in this way.

When he had finished his breakfast, the man woke his wife, said goodbye, and went off to the hills to cut wood. On his way out the door, the man reminded the bird to check on his wife and make sure she got out of bed.

The man's wife was ill-tempered and lazy. Her husband was naturally an early riser and a hard worker, but one other reason he left so early and worked so late every day may have been to be free from his sharp-tongued wife for as long as possible.

As the farmer had asked, the sparrow went in to make sure the woman was awake to begin the day. As usual, however, she was still asleep. The sun was high in the sky before the woman heeded the sparrow's calls to get up and get on with the day's chores.

She made a simple breakfast in the kitchen, but unlike the old man, she did not offer anything to the sparrow. She hated the bird, because her husband gave it so much attention. In her mind, he treated the bird like it was the child they never had, and she resented anything — even a bird — getting more attention than she.

After finishing breakfast, she made some starch, gathered all the dirty clothes in their tiny home into one great bundle, put the bundle on her back, and set off for the river to do her laundry.

"Watch over the house to make sure nothing strange happens," she told the bird.

The bird had not had breakfast yet, and there was no food in her food bowl. She mentioned this to the old woman, but the impatient

SHITAKIRI SUZUME

woman ignored her. "Oh, and leave the starch alone," she said as she left for the river.

The bird was hungry, but she tried to put her hunger out of her mind by distracting herself. She flew about the house, practicing the acrobatic tricks the old man had taught her, but soon these activities gave way to hunger and she flew back to the kitchen.

The old woman had ignored her empty food dish, and there was nothing at all to eat. "Except," thought the sparrow, "the starch. But the woman is doing laundry and will need the starch later, will she not? I should not eat the starch."

But the sparrow's little stomach soon began grumbling and growling like a beast within the bird. The sparrow flew over to the table, landed by the plate of starch and looked at it.

"It's so full," though the hungry sparrow. "There's so much there. Even if I eat a little bit, there will still be enough for the old woman to do her laundry."

With that thought, the sparrow pecked at the starch on the plate. She pecked a little more and a little more until she had eaten half the plate. It wasn't that the starch was particularly tasty — indeed, it tasted as one might expect — dry and powdery. But the bird had eaten half of the plate before she realized she had done so. Now she knew there was going to be trouble.

When the old woman returned she did not enter the kitchen. She went straight to the back yard, where she spread the clothes on a board so they would dry flat, without wrinkles. After she had spread all the clothes out this way she went into the kitchen for the starch.

"Bird?" she bellowed in her high voice. "Bird! Where are you? Did you do this? Did you eat the starch?"

The bird sheepishly fluttered up from the far corner and said, "Yes, I ate the starch."

The old woman began seething, waiting to explode into a rage. Her ears were deaf to the sparrow's explanations.

"But I didn't mean to eat so much of it. I was hungry, and you seemed to have overlooked my food dish. I know it was no fault of your own, but — "

"Bird!" screamed the old woman in a frenzy. "How can I do laundry without starch? What did you expect me to do when I came home with a huge bundle of clean, wet clothes and found the starch all gone?"

"I did not eat it *all*. There's some left."

"Don't talk back to me, bird." The woman was lost in rage as her mind counted off innumerable slights, real and imaginary, she had suffered because of the bird.

She chased the bird into a corner of the kitchen and grabbed her. Holding her tightly, she looked for the closest thing with which to punish her. "The scissors!" she thought, and grabbed a pair of garden scissors from beneath the table.

"This will teach you to do as your told, bird!" The old woman pried open the little bird's beak and cut out her tongue. When she had finished, she threw the bird at the wall.

The bird bounced off the wall and, unable to fly because of the pain, landed on the floor with her wings spread apart. The woman moved closer and raised her foot to step on the bird, but the bird recovered enough to fly away. The woman cursed as her foot struck only the floor. Chirping in pain, the sparrow disappeared into the sky.

The old man came home from the fields at his usual time. He greeted his wife, who asked how his day was.

This puzzled the man. "Why do you ask? You've never listened before when I've told you about my work."

"You look tired and I was worried about you."

As his wife had rarely shown him anything but contempt, the old man knew something was wrong. He looked around the house to see if anything was out of order, but he found nothing out of the ordinary. Then, looking for his companion, the sparrow, he asked his wife, "Where is my little friend?"

"I don't know, dear." The old woman's voice was sweet and cheery. "She must be out playing somewhere. Or perhaps she's left you. You know how those animals will turn on you. No matter how kind you are to them, no matter how you take care of them, they'll all leave you in the end, won't they?"

The man was worried, and ate little of his supper when the woman laid the table. He continued worrying about the sparrow even after they had gone to bed.

"Was she unhappy because I did not feed her this morning?" he wondered. "Have I done something to hurt her? Why would she leave me?"

Before long, the man gave way to tears. That he would cry over something she though so trivial angered the old woman, and she broke down and told him what had really happened.

The man was very upset. He had known his wife had many, many shortcomings, but he had tried not to think of her as cruel and heartless. But now there was no other way to look at what she had done. She had tried to kill his only friend, and though she failed, she had maimed his companion and chased her from the house. The man was distraught, and spent the night weeping in the kitchen. The woman ignored him and slept.

The next morning the man awoke at his usual early hour. Instead of going to work as usual, however, he packed a lunch and went to look for the sparrow.

He walked through the hills where he had first met the bird long ago, crying as he went.

"Sparrow, sparrow. Come to me, my friend. I am sorry my wife did such a horrendous thing to you. I am sorry I was not there to protect you. I am sorry...."

He went from hill to hill until he reached the foot of a mountain. He climbed up the mountain, still crying for his lost bird to come to him, but there came no reply. Finally, around noon he sat down to eat his lunch. It was then that by chance a small sparrow — the man could tell on sight that it was not his sparrow — came and lighted on a branch ear him.

"Hello, sparrow. Do you know what has become of my friend? She is a sparrow like you, but my wife cut her tongue out. I am looking for my friend to apologize to her, and tell her how sorry I am."

The little sparrow flew down to where the man was sitting and spoke to him. "You are the old man? We have heard everything from your friend. How did you marry such a woman? That is of no matter. I will lead you to your friend."

The man was happy to hear this, and offered the bird some of his rice ball, which the bird gratefully accepted. Then the bird took to the skies with the old man following close behind.

After about an hour of walking trough dense brush, the bird stopped and pointed to a wooden house a short distance away.

"Wait here while I speak with your friend," said the bird, and it flew to the house.

The man stood where he was, and shortly his sparrow came out of the house. He recognized his friend at once, and was startled to see her in the fine silk robes of a princess. Something had happened to change her, it seemed. Either he had been reduced to the size of a sparrow, or his friend had grown to human size! The man was puzzled, but he was so happy to see his companion he forgot about their sizes.

He dropped to his knees before his friend and bowed his head in apology. "I am sorry, my friend of so many years. Please forgive my wife

SHITAKIRI SUZUME 95

what she has done, and me for not protecting you better."

"Rise, my friend. You have no need to bow your head before me. I have grown a new tongue, as you can see, and I am doing well. But I am touched that you would come to find me. And I am very happy to see you again. Have you eaten?"

The sparrow waved a wing and led him into the house, where she showed him to a grand hall where three sparrows sat before him. Like the old man's companion, these sparrows were also wearing robes showing great rank and nobility. The old man bowed deeply, and his friend motioned for him to sit with them.

"Your wife injured our princess most gravelly," said the largest of the birds in a voice rich with anger. "We would — "

Another bird raised a wing to silence him, and spoke in his place. "You have been our lady's companion for many years. You have cared for her as if she were your own child, and loved her with all our heart. She has told us of your kindness, and she loves you deeply as well. Any human winning the favor of our princess of course has our favor as well. You are welcome here. We would like to have a feast in your honor. Please, enjoy yourself, and entertain yourself as you will."

He waved a wing, and three smaller sparrows brought out trays filled with food. The old man's friend sat next to him, and they talked of old times and memories they shared together. The other sparrows had heard of the man's kindness, and they were very happy to meet him after having heard so much about him for so long.

The man ate his fill, and talked with his friend until the sky began to grow dark.

"I am sorry. I have enjoyed my stay here, but I must be going. Already I will return later than the usual time, and I know my wife will have harsh words for me."

"Indeed, indeed," said his friend. "But we would like to give you a gift. I will never return to your home as your pet, but I would like to give you something to remember me by."

A door slid open and two sparrows laid two boxes, one large, the other smaller, on the floor.

"Please choose one box to take with you as a gift. Choose whichever you wish, but do not open the box until you are home."

The man thanked her, but he declined to choose. "I really don't need a gift to remember you by. You are etched in my heart, my friend."

But the sparrows insisted, and in the end the man choose the smaller box. I am an old man, and the large box looks too heavy to carry all the way home. This will be fine, thank you."

The man said his goodbyes, and the sparrows flew with the man for the extent of the dense brush. There they left him, and turned back to fly home.

The old man returned home. As he had expected, his wife complained of his late return, but she fell silent when her husband put the box on the table.

"What, what is this?" she asked.

The man told her how he went looking for his

friend to apologize, and how he had been led to the home where the sparrow lived. He told her how the sparrow was some sort of magical bird, that she had regrown the tongue his wife had so cruelly cut out. More, he told her, the sparrow was a princess, some sort of royalty among the animals of the wilds.

The woman touched her head to gesture he was babbling like a lunatic. "So what's in the box?" she asked impatiently.

"Let's see."

The man slid the latch open, then slowly lifted the lid of the box. The old man and his wife were blinded momentarily, as the light in the kitchen was reflected and magnified countless times. The box was full of gold and precious gems — diamonds, emeralds, rubies and more!

The man was silent in reflection. His sparrow — the princess — loved him so much she gave him these jewels! There was enough treasure for him and his wife to live comfortably for the rest of their lives!

His wife was also happy, and forgot her spiteful tongue for some time. Soon, however, she grew angry.

"Why didn't you take the larger box? That would have made us even wealthier. It would have been full of even more gold and jewels. Pah, what a fool I have married.

"Tomorrow morning I'll go get the bigger box. It should be ours, you know — you just took the wrong one."

The man was disappointed, but ignored her as she complained and complained late into the night.

The next morning the woman awoke early. Her husband set out for the hills to cut wood as usual. He was not ready to stop his work just because he was now a wealthy man. Not yet, he thought.

The old woman went looking for the sparrow. She was deep in the mountains and thoroughly lost when she decided to sit down and eat her lunch. Like her husband, she had packed a rice ball for her meal, and as she ate it she saw a sparrow watching her from a branch above her head.

"Hello, sparrow," she said.

The sparrow said nothing.

"Perhaps you could help me. I am looking for a sparrow that had its tongue cut out."

The sparrow remained silent, but fluttered down to the ground in front of the woman. It pecked at the ground as if looking for food. The woman saw this, but she greedily stuffed the last of her rice ball into her mouth, leaving none for the bird. The bird saw this, and looked the woman in the eyes for a moment. Then it took flight.

The woman rose and followed, and the sparrow stopped, waiting until the woman caught up. The sparrow kept flying a little bit, then waiting for the woman to catch up, and the old woman was sure the bird was leading her to the sparrows' home. But her husband hadn't mentioned the sparrow leading him through brambles, briars, thorns and thistles as she was now being led. Nor did she remember her husband mentioning a stream, but he sparrow led her across — through — several streams until finally, wet and her skin torn by thorns and thistles, she saw a house nearby.

Without waiting to be invited in, the woman burst through the door and into the great hall, where she found four sparrows sitting peacefully.

"Greetings, my lady," said the sparrow, the old man's companion.

"Good day. I would stay for the feast, but I have no time to dawdle. I believe you offered my husband a box larger than the one he took home. I have come to claim the larger box, as he meant to take the larger one, but his eyesight is not what it used to be, you know, and he took the smaller one by mistake.

"The larger box now, if you will."

"As you wish, my lady," said the sparrow princess. She waved to another bird, which disappeared into another room.

One of the princess' retainers rose and spoke. "Why, why did you cut my lady's tongue out? What cruelty could have possessed you to harm a bird, a sparrow?"

The princess turned to her retainer and told him, "Silence. The lady is a guest in our home now, and must be treated as such."

"Thank you," said the old woman. "I will overlook your retainers unpleasantness."

The sparrow princess was irritated by the woman's tone, but she smiled when a door slid open and another sparrow brought the old woman the box.

"And without further delay I will be off," said the woman as she struggled to get the box strapped on her back. "Thank you, indeed."

The birds assembled and bowed to the woman as she teetered and tottered out of the house and back through the woods. The weight of the great box was such that she had a difficult time keeping her balance for more than a few steps, and she had to stop frequently.

She heeded her husband's words that the birds had told him not to open the box until he had returned home, but each time she stopped to rest she found herself more and more tempted to open it. Finally, after a few hours of struggling to carry the great box through the woods, she stopped again. This time she decided she should open the box.

"Those birds. What if they are playing a trick on us? I should open the box now. The birds never said anything to *me* about not opening the box."

She turned the box to face her. Slowly, she slid the wooden latch and opened the lid, and as soon as the lid had opened a horde of demons, skeletons, goblins and other monsters jumped out at her!

It was horrible! A great demon with fiery red eyes stared at the woman as a skeleton tried to grab her. Rats and mice, flies and roaches and other insects streamed out of the box in droves, circling around her as she cowered in fear. She had never dreamed of monsters as ferocious or frightening as these, and here they were, all waiting to take her as their own.

The woman turned and ran as fast as she could. She did not stop — not even to catch her breath — until she got home.

After she had recovered, the woman told her husband the story — omitting points such as her rudeness to the sparrows — and told him to take his axe and go kill them all. The old man, though, told her the sparrows were not to blame.

The woman thought about his words, and before long she came to agree with him that it had all been caused by her greed and anger. She and her husband spent the rest of their lives living in the greatest comfort, free from hunger and want, because of the treasures in the smaller box.

Over time, the woman mended her ways, and by the time of her death she died a kind, agreeable old lady. (The process is said to have taken a considerable amount of time.)

Sannin Kyōdai — The Three Brothers

Long ago there lived a man with a beautiful wife and three young sons. He had an older brother, and the two brothers made it a point of pride to compete with each other in everything they did. As a result, both men were fabulously wealthy. However, the competitive drive that built each man's fortune was also a weakness. The two spent most of their time adding to their fortunes, and other aspects of life were, well, wanting.

The younger brother's life was so devoted to increasing his fortune that he could not be troubled to marry or produce offspring. Indeed, he was often so absorbed in the wheeling and dealing within his financial empire that he had to be reminded, even persuaded at times, to eat.

The first wealthy man had found the time to marry and marry well. His bride was not only the only daughter of a family with great political power, but she was also one of the most beautiful women in the land. But despite her beauty, her husband spent so much time managing his estate that his sons found that from time to time they forgot what their father looked like.

The way the man named his sons provides an excellent illustration of his lack of concern with family matters. The birth of their first son was a source of great joy for the man, for his beautiful wife had given him an heir. In his elation, the wealthy man spent great amounts of money on celebrations marking the boy's birth. He named the boy Taro, using the characters for "fat" and "male." To most readers this might not seem a very flattering choice of names. However, it is a common enough name in Japan, and if you feel like forgiving the man for naming his son with characters that could be read "fat boy" you may prefer to think of the name as meaning "bountiful man" or "blessed man."

Soon after Taro's birth, the man's wife gave birth to a second child. Another celebration ensued, though on something of a subdued scale when compared to the festivities accompanying the birth of Taro. The second child was of lesser importance to the wealthy man, and he named the child Jiro. Like Taro, Jiro is a common name in Japan. But again, the characters that make up Jiro do not seem very flattering to the Western reader: the characters mean "next" and "male." (In defence of those who have chosen to name their second sons "Jiro," Japanese readers may question the originality many Westerners show in naming their children after themselves: John Smith, Junior; Bill Brown III; Louis XIV and so on.)

A yet smaller celebration followed the birth

of the third child, who received the rather uninspired name Saburo, consisting of the characters for "third" and "male."

After the birth of the third child the man decided his family was taking too much of his time. He shut himself in his offices for days on end, working late into the night, counting his gold and adding to it little by little until his huge fortune was even greater than before.

By the time his three sons made the transformation from boys to men, their father was one of the wealthiest men in their land. The boys felt very proud of their father, though they saw him only rarely. They grew up in lavish style, eating the finest foods and wearing the finest robes that money could buy. They were not lazy, by any means, for their father had seen to it they were raised in a strict fashion. He made sure the boys would be able to fend for themselves should the need ever arise.

When the wealthy man decided the time was appropriate, he called the boys together for a meeting in the garden of his great estate.

"Your uncle and I," the man began, "earned everything you see around you all by ourselves." Accustomed to being surrounded by those who hung on his every word, the man paused dramatically to let his words sink in.

The three boys, unaccustomed to seeing their father, not to mention hearing him speak, blinked at the wealthy man in response.

"Yes, we built it all," the father continued.

"And we built it, we built it because we were men. Real men. We woke up early and worked late into the night. When something needed to be done, by golly we did it, right then and there."

Jiro tried and failed to swallow a yawn, prompting his father to come to the point of his address. "I am an old man. I will not live much longer, and I want to spend the little life I have left enjoying the fruits of my labor.

"My sons, I will give one of you my estate. I will keep a small part of what I own — enough to enjoy myself in my old age — but I will give the rest to one, and only one of you. The other two of you will have nothing."

The boys looked at each other with great surprise, a response that pleased their father.

"Yes, one of you. I have not decided which of you will win this vast empire. No, no. You will compete for it, like my brother and I competed to build our fortunes. However, the competition I have in mind is somewhat different than the years of struggle my brother and I endured for our fortunes. The three of you are hereby banished from this home and from all my lands for one year. After the year passes, you may return.

"Spend the year however you like, but be advised. The one of you that spends his time in what I decide is the wisest manner possible will win my entire fortune. The two of you that fail will have nothing."

Before the boys could recover, the old man wordlessly left the room. The boys looked at each other in shock.

"Does he mean this?" asked Saburo.

Before either of his brothers could reply, their father's guards appeared in the garden and told the boys they had to leave. The boys were escorted to the door, where each was given a change of clothing, a blanket and a tiny amount of money.

The boys walked away from their family home in confusion. Their confusion soon turned to resignation, and when fate conspired to present them with a fork in the road that led off in three different directions, they knew they would have to separate and live on their own for a year.

Promising to meet again next year on the first day of the fifth month, each boy set out on a different path. Saburo took the trail to the far right, which led toward the sea, and Jiro took the middle trail, which crossed the plains and disappeared into the distance. Taro was left with the path to the right, which went up into the mountains.

Taro walked along the trail until sunset. Just as Taro cleared a spot of ground on which to lay his blanket, it began to rain. The rain increased in intensity until it was a terrible storm. Thunder deafened Taro, lightning blinded him, and a relentless, icy rain soaked him to the bone. Then, after what seemed like hours, the storm suddenly dissipated.

Taro was dazed for several moments. He wondered what to do. He was wet and cold, and there was no place to sleep save the muddy earth. Bewildered, he began looked around him for a flat stretch of solid ground on which to sleep. As he looked, something off in the distance caught his eye. "A light!" he thought, but he remembered he had had a terrible evening thus far, and it was likely that the cold was playing tricks of his thunder-and-lightning dazzled brain.

He closed his eyes and rubbed them, thinking deliberately of other things. Yet when he opened his eyes once more the light was still there, dancing in the distance.

Thinking that it was a sign of some sort, Taro began making his way toward the source of the light. He soon discovered that the light was not on the trail. He passed through brambles and briars which tore at his skin as he passed, and he climbed over or crept under many great trees felled by the storm. When at last he reached the source of the light, he found it was coming from within a house built into the mountain. But what kind of person would live here, off the trail in the middle of the mountains?

Summoning his courage, Taro knocked on the door. No one answered his knock, so he knocked again, louder. This produced a reply, as a voice from deep within the home yelled something unintelligible.

The door was opened by an old woman.

She said nothing as she took him by the hand and led him in. Then she handed him a towel, and as he towelled himself off she spoke her first words to him.

"I've been expecting you," she said in a voice that reminded Taro of the whistle on a boiling kettle of tea.

Taro did his best to remain composed. He continued to dry himself, then said, "I only want a place to stay the night."

"The night?" laughed the old woman. "You can stay as long as you like."

Taro lowered his guard a bit. He would continue on his way at dawn and —

"But in return, you must collect some firewood for me," the woman spoke again. She pointed to a small scythe on the wall. "As long as the blade on that hand scythe is sharp, you cannot leave."

Lightning flashed silently, then the accompanying boom of thunder shattered the air.

"I accept your terms," Taro said haltingly.

Things went better than Taro had anticipated that first night. The old woman, who he learned was in fact a mountain witch, took care of him and fed him. He woke with the sun and collected all the wood and grass he could carry. When he could not find dead and dried wood or grasses, he used the scythe to cut saplings and green branches and grass, which he then dried in the sun.

Over time, Taro became a proficient woodsman, and he came to enjoy his life in the woods. But the year was coming to an end before he knew it. Soon he would have to leave and return to his home.

When he mentioned his impending departure to the mountain witch, she told him sternly, "Not until the blade of your scythe has dulled. Only when it can cut no more will you be free to leave."

This, Taro knew, was not likely. He believed the mountain witch had used her powers to put some sort of spell on the blade, for no matter how hard he worked, no matter how many fields of grass he cut and no matter how many saplings he chopped down, the blade remained in pristine condition. If he waited for the blade to dull through normal wear and tear, he knew he could very well be a guest of the mountain witch for the rest of his days. But rather than confront the witch with this, Taro said nothing and went back to work.

As he worked, cutting grass high on a mountain plateau, Taro thought of the blade again. How could he dull it enough to free him from his agreement with the old woman? As he pondered his possibilities, he heard a voice speak to him. "The rocks. Use those rocks."

Taro spun around. Who could have crept up on him without his hearing it? And who could have known his thoughts? Was this more of the witch's magic? No one was there. He walked around the small plateau and found he was alone. Aside from his own footprints, there was no sign that anyone had climbed up to the plateau by the trail. But he had heard the voice as if it had been within his own head. Puzzled, Taro returned to his work.

When the sun began to drop behind the hills, Taro picked up his bundles of grass and started down the trail. But, remembering the voice, he dropped his bundles and took the hand scythe from his belt. Without expectations, he brought the sharp blade down on a jagged boulder that stuck out from the mountain.

Ssssshhhhka The blade cut through the rock. He tried again on a larger boulder, and again the blade went through the stone with no difficulties. But when he pressed the blade against a third boulder, the scythe passed cleanly through half of the stone, then it got stuck.

Taro tugged at the scythe several times, and only after the most strenuous exertions did he manage to free the blade from the stone. However, his joy at having rescued his only tool was doubled when he saw what the stone had to the blade — it was dull! In some places it was cracked and broken.

Taro gathered his bundles of grass and raced back to the witch's cabin. She was not displeased with him, and cooked a grand dinner to mark his final night as her guest.

Taro awoke at dawn the next day. After breakfast he packed his small bundle of things and was preparing to leave when the mountain witch came to him with a straw doll in her hand. The doll depicted a smiling young boy.

"I'm sorry this is all I have to give you," she said, pressing the doll into his hand. "After all you've done I would have liked to give you something greater, but . . . "

Taro thanked her, wrapped the doll in cloth and tucked it into his shirt. Then he waved goodbye, and headed through the forest on his way home.

The trail led Taro back to his hometown. The first thing he noticed when he reached the town was how hungry he was. The breakfast the mountain witch's had prepared seemed to have disappeared from his stomach as if it had been one of the old woman's magical pranks.

To further tease his empty belly, he arrived at the village just before lunch time. With each step he took the smell of cooking food grew stronger. But when Taro reached into his pockets, he found they were empty.

"What am I to do," Taro muttered to himself.

"Leave it to me," a voice replied.

Embarrassed that he had spoken his thoughts so frankly, Taro turned to see who had overheard him. No one was to his left, no one was to his right, and there was no one behind him.

"I'm here," the voice spoke again, "in your bundle."

"The doll?" thought Taro? He stepped into a small copse of trees and took the bundle from his breast. Unrolling the bundle, he saw that the doll was moving.

"Just leave it to me, okay?"

Taro nodded, and before he could react, the doll had jumped up and disappeared. Not sure what to believe, Taro just sat there under the trees for a few moments. When finally he decided he had been hallucinating (due to his great hunger, of course), the doll returned.

"Check behind that tree," it said, pointing to the tree closest to the path. Taro did as the doll asked, and discovered a plate of grilled fish (salmon — his favorite kind) and a heaping bowl of rice! Thanking the doll, Taro pounced on the food and ate every last morsel. When he finished, he found that the doll had returned to its normal state and was once again just an ordinary, lifeless straw doll.

Taro carefully wrapped the doll in cloth and once again tucked it safely in his shirt. Then, with a full belly, he went back to the trail and continued his walk home.

When Taro came to the point where the three roads merged into one, he found his brothers waiting for his as they had promised. But both Jiro and Saburo were different. They had all left wearing rough clothes and with only a small amount of money, but both of his brothers were garbed in the most splendid robes and accompanied by tens of armed men, servants and other followers. Tents of brilliant colors had been pitched, as it became clear that both brothers had made great fortunes in their year away from home.

Jiro and Saburo were surprised to find their older brother was not at least as successful as they had become, but they concealed their disappointment well. They welcomed their brother warmly, and together the three brothers returned to their family home.

On his sons' return, the father welcomed everyone with a great feast and varied entertainments. Then, as the climax of the evening, the father led the crowd into the great garden, where called his sons before the crowd and asked them in turn what they had learned in the year.

The wealthy man asked his youngest son to speak first. The heretofore shy and reserved Saburo stepped before the crowd and spoke with more poise than anyone had thought possible.

"I have studied the way of the bow," said Saburo. He notched an arrow and drew a great bow. Then he aimed at an object off in the distance. Night had fallen, and the assembled crowd was not sure what target Saburo had chosen, but the youngest son let the arrow fly and then quickly called out, "The torches!"

Quickly he notched another arrow and again

he drew the great bow. Just as he sent the second arrow speeding on its way, a torch flickering in the distance winked out. The crowd murmured its respect, but Saburo had already launched a third arrow. A second torch winked out, and then the third. In the blink of an eye, Saburo had extinguished three torches at a considerable distance.

"You have shown your proficiency with the bow, my son," said the father. "And this entourage you have put together shows me what it has brought you. You have done well."

Then the father pointed to Jiro, who stood and waved to a retainer. The retainer brought him a *katana*, which Jiro drew and allowed the crowd to inspect. It was a Muromatsu *katana*, of the finest quality, and his mere possession of such a blade earned Jiro the crowd's respect, as only the greatest swordsmen were allowed to wield weapons made by the Muromatsu.

Jiro waved the crowd to step away from him, and a retainer threw a number of squares of paper into the air. With scarcely a whisper, the fine Muromatsu blade cut the air, and when Jiro had finished, the ten squares of paper had been cut into sixty tiny pieces of paper, each as perfectly square as the other.

The crowd gasped at the display of swordsmanship, and the father congratulated Jiro on his skill. "Most impressive, my son. You have spent your time well."

Then it was Taro's turn. He stood and wondered what he was going to say. "I can't say I have become a master of gathering wood and drying grass," he thought to himself.

The crowd parted as he approached his father. As he neared the wealthy man, Taro heard the voice of the doll whisper to him. "Tell them you have become the finest thief in all the land."

Taro stood before the crowd and did as the doll suggested: "I have become the finest thief in all the land!"

The crowd gasped as one, and Taro's father jumped from his seat. "You *what*? You've become the finest what, you say?"

Taro mind reeled. "*Thief*, right?" he thought, "The doll told me to say I was the finest *thief* in the land, right? I did *not* misunderstand, did I?" The doll said nothing more. In a meeker voice, Taro repeated himself. "I have become the finest thief in all the land."

His father's face paled and the old man exploded with rage. "You are not my son! My sons are all honorable men, fine citizens of this land! You, you . . ." The man was unable to express his anger in words.

Shaking his fist, Taro's father gave his oldest son an icy glare and said, "You are banished from this house! Should you darken my doorway again, it will be all I can do to keep the guards from killing you as — as the thief you are! Take a horse, and go as far from here as you can!"

The old man stormed out of the garden. The

crowd dispersed. Taro's brothers looked at him with pity, but they said nothing as they followed their father. At last, only Taro, his father's guards and his uncle were left.

"Let's go, young master," said one of the guards. His voice still expressed the respect he felt for Taro and his family, but he was bound to obey his master's commands and expel Taro from the garden.

"Wait," said Taro's uncle. "I would like a word with the master thief." The guards assented, and Taro and his uncle sat down.

Taro's uncle was, like his father, incredibly wealthy. He was a gruff man who kept to himself, but he could be warm and generous on occasion. In the back of his mind, Taro thought the childless uncle was thinking of adopting the now orphaned Taro as his own son.

"The finest thief in all the land, eh?" asked the uncle with a laugh.

Taro cast his eyes downward and answered glumly, "Yes, the finest thief in all the land."

"Well, thief Taro, a claim like that needs some proof to back it up. If you are not the finest thief in all the land, then you have gotten yourself thrown out of your home for no good reason. But if you are the finest thief in the land, you will never need a home again, will you? You will be able to steal anything you need, whenever you need it no?"

Taro nodded.

"So show me, thief. Show me your skills. Do

you remember the T'ang Dynasty pin I like to wear?" The uncle was given to common, ordinary, inexpensive clothing, but his one concession to his vanity was an impressive jade pin he acquired in his dealings with traders from China.

"Yes," Taro said. "Have you lost it? I notice you are not wearing it tonight."

"I was in such a hurry to visit my brother and celebrate the return of his three sons," the uncle winked at Taro, "I forgot to put it on today. Do you think, master thief, you could get it for me?"

Taro heard the doll's voice whisper to his from the bundle in his breast. "Of course you can."

"Certainly," replied Taro.

"Excellent," smiled the uncle. "Well, it is unguarded and in my home. Anyone could get it. However, a master thief like you should be able to get it while, say, you are in conversation here with me, don't you agree?"

"Do you mean I should get the pendant from your home in Bancho, four *ri* away, while I am here talking with you?"

"That is exactly what I mean."

Taro heard the doll whisper again, "No problem. You can get it, you can get it."

"I'll have it for you shortly," beamed Taro.

Taro and his uncle talked of the events of the past year. They talked, Taro distractedly, of who had been married, who had died, how the uncle's various business ventures had fared and so on. After fifteen minutes or so, Taro's pocket suddenly felt heavier. Taro put his hand in his pocket and, to his uncle's surprise, pulled out the jade T'ang pin.

"I am impressed, young thief," said the uncle. "Well done."

Taro only smiled in reply.

"But," continued the uncle, "as I said, anyone could get it. It was unguarded in my home and I told you where to find it. How about a real test?

"Tonight I will prepare two chests of gold. They will be somewhere on my estate. I will have any number of guards ready and waiting to catch a thief, but if you are as good as you say you are, if you are the finest thief in the land, they will never know you have been there until you have disappeared with enough gold to make you a very wealthy man for the rest of your life.

"The gold is insured. I am very wary of thieves and have insured everything of value in my home. This means, my thieving nephew, that if you steal anything from me, it is no particular loss to me. You may keep it. If you are caught, however, you must be dealt with accordingly. My insurers would be very suspicious if I caught a thief in my home, then let him go without the proper punishment.

"But the finest thief in all the land should have no trouble, eh? What do you say, thief? If you win, you join the ranks of the idle rich. If you fail, you meet the fate of all thieves."

"Agree! Agree!" whispered the doll in a shrill voice.

"I accept the challenge."

Taro's uncle returned to his estate and began preparations right away. As promised, he had two great chests filled with gold. The chests were locked in his storeroom and guards were posted at the doorway. More guards were posted at strategic points throughout the estate, and all were warned that someone was going to try to steal their master's gold that night.

Next, the uncle assembled all the children on the estate and told them they were responsible for lighting torches and fires when they heard the alarm. He ordered all the young boys to be ready with flint stones and fuel. When the guards sounded the alarm, the boys were to strike the flints and start fires to make sure the thief would not disappear in the darkness.

To assist the boys, the master issued hollow bamboo pipes to the young girls of the estate. When the boys had lit small fires, the girls would blow through the pipes to feed the fires and help them burn brighter.

Confident in his defenses, Taro's uncle went to sleep early that night. His last thoughts before he drifted off to sleep were, "If he can breach my defenses, he deserves the gold."

As Taro and the straw doll made their way to the uncle's home, the doll produced a small bag.

"These are my tools," he said, slinging the bag over his shoulder. When Taro asked to see them, the doll opened the bag and showed him a great collection of miniature musical instruments. There were tiny bells, flutes, a drum and more. Taro was surprised, but he did not question the doll. "Whatever happens," he thought, "the doll seems to know what it is doing."

Taro dismounted from the horse well before he came to the gates of his uncle's estate. Quietly, he slipped across the land to the estate's outer wall.

"Just let me go in first," whispered the straw doll. "When I'm ready, I'll come get you."

Taro nodded, and the doll disappeared into the night.

The doll first visited the children's quarters, where he found everyone asleep. Quietly, he took one of the tiny bells from his bag. Waving his hand over it, the doll recited a spell, whereupon the tiny bell grew in size until it became a normal-sized bell. He did the same with all the other bells, then with all the bamboo flutes.

Carefully and silently, he crept from child to child and replaced all their tools with musical instruments. For the boys, he replaced their flints with bells; for the girls, he replaced their bamboo pipes with bamboo flutes.

Quickly, the doll rushed from the children's quarters to the uncle's bedroom. There, the doll pulled two tiny drums from his bag. Enlarging them, he put the drums to the left and right of his master's feet. Next, he moved the uncle's sword from his bedside, and replaced it with a drumstick.

Next, the doll rushed to the storehouse where the two great chests of gold were kept. Here, the doll waved his hand over himself. Speaking magic words, he made himself so small he could not be seen. He crept past the guards at the storehouse, then he climbed up the storehouse door. When he reached the lock, he crawled inside the keyhole and unlocked the locks from within.

Then, the tiny doll slipped back past the guards and returned to the wall where an anxious Taro was waiting for him.

"It's all set," he told Taro. "We only have to wait a few moments."

Taro's uncle had an awful dream. In his dream, his nightmare, a thief was stealing all his gold. In his dream, all his retainers were worthless fools, the best of whom had trouble catching his breath, not to mention a thief. But still, he had single-handedly cornered the thief, and was now chasing him across his estate.

As he dreamed, Taro's uncle stirred violently in his sleep, and rolled from side to side in his nightmare. He kicked his legs as if he really was running after the thief. Somewhere in his dreams, it sounded like someone was beating a great drum.

At the wall, Taro was surprised to hear a dull *thud-thud, thud* sound come from the estate. Someone was sounding the alarm, he thought. The game was over. It would only be a matter of time before he was caught.

But the doll was not surprised. Instead, he told Taro, "Go on, help yourself to two chests of gold!"

Taro did as he was advised and climbed over the gate.

The guards at Taro's uncle's estate were keen and watchful. Their swords were sharp and their ears were alert for the first sound of an alarm. That a thief would have the audacity to try and rob their master's estate — and to go so far as to warn the master in advance he would be robbed — this was too much for their pride. They swore they would punish the thief severely when they caught him, and they vowed the gold was safe in their care.

So when they heard the alarm drum, they converged on the source of the sound without a moment's hesitation. They located the source easily, and they quickly surrounded the uncle's quarters. The thief would not escape them.

Taro watched as all the guards left the storeroom and raced toward his uncle's quarters. The storeroom was thus unguarded, and it was no challenge for Taro to walk into the undefended, unlocked storeroom and help himself to two chests brimming with gold. in fact, it was much

JAPANESE FAIRY TALES

more of a challenge for Taro to try to carry two great chests than it was to get them, but the straw doll solved this problem with another wave of his hand and more magic words. The two chests shrank to a tiny size. Taro scooped up the chests and, putting one in each pocket of his jacket, raced to the wall and his waiting horse. The straw doll shrank himself to his normal size. Taro put him back in the bundle, which he then tucked back into his shirt. Thus done, Taro spurred his horse and rode off into the hills.

A group of the biggest, strongest guards went in to catch the thief, their swords drawn and their faces set in angry masks. They were met at the stairs by their master, who was waving a drumstick in the air and screaming, "He's not *here* you fools! What are you doing here? The gold! You should be guarding the gold!"

But the master's words were downed out as the air exploded in musical cacophony. When the children heard the alarm they rushed to perform their various fire-starting duties. The boys struck what they thought were flints, and the countryside echoed with the peal of bells. When the girls blew their bamboo pipes to feed the fires that had been prepared earlier, the air was alive with scores of bamboo flutes.

The strange symphony confused the guards, who could not hear their superiors issuing new orders. Each guard seemed to have an idea where the thief was, and all the guards ran off in different directions.

Taro's uncle, knowing his gold was gone, held his head in his hands and sighed. Tomorrow he would have to meet with his insurers.

Taro heard the odd music as his horse galloped away. He didn't know what it was, but he knew it was the doll's doing. He looked back once and smiled. Then he put his head down and guided his horse into the night.

Taro never used his "thieving skills" after the night he made his fortune. Over the years, he acquired a reputation as something of an eccentric because he always kept a plain straw doll on a special shelf in his home, a great mansion on a sprawling countryside estate. Like his father and his uncle, Taro was a very wealthy man.

Bakemonodera — The Monk and the Evil Temple

The monk stood in the doorway as the old woman filled his begging bowl with food.

The woman filled his bowl and smiled as she returned it. "Vegetables, some rice and a special soft rice cake, because it's been so long since we've had a monk in these parts."

"What about the temple I saw on my way into town? I was thinking of staying the night there tonight."

"Oh, you couldn't possibly stay there," said the woman.

"Why would they refuse a fellow monk a night's stay?"

"It's not that you would be refused. Oh, no. You could stay there all right. But over the years who knows how many young priests have been sent out to the temple and all of them — every single one of them — they've all turned up dead! Awful! Throats torn open as if by some wild animal."

Tasuke, the monk, nodded to signal the woman to continue.

"It's haunted! Some demon is there, waiting to kill anyone who dares visit the place."

"But how do you . . ."

The woman cut him off in mid-sentence. "If it weren't for wandering priests like you, we would never have a proper funeral in these parts. No one has been to that temple in years."

The monk Tasuke thought to himself for a moment. "A temple without a priest. And I am a monk without a temple. This is a calling, and how am I to refuse it. All I have to do is live long enough."

He turned to the woman and proclaimed, "I will end these hauntings and become your priest. I will become the priest of the haunted temple."

"No, you can't do that!" the woman cried. "You'll end up like all the others who wouldn't listen. I tried to warn them, but they wouldn't listen. Not a one of them. Fools."

The foolishness of so many young monks gone to their doom angered the woman, and she angrily drew a finger across her throat from one side to the other. "If you must go, mind your throat!"

The garden surrounding the temple had not been tended for some years, but the temple itself looked to be in good condition. Tasuke received no answer when he stood at the entrance and called out, *"Konban wa,* Good evening," so he entered and began looking around.

A voice booming out from behind him startled him so that he almost dropped his bowl. "A traveler! Welcome, welcome. I am Goro, the priest of this temple."

Tasuke turned and faced a tall, muscular man with sharply drawn features. Though the woman made no mention of anyone living at the temple, the man was in the robes of a head priest. The priest's size and apparent strength was such that had the two met in different circumstances, Tasuke would have taken him for a woodsman or laborer. Smiling, he introduced himself. "I am Tasuke, the traveler."

The priest introduced himself. "Well met, well met! But a traveler? Your robes and bowl tell me you are a priest. You have not been assigned to this temple?"

"Sadly, no, though I had heard this temple was without a priest."

"A temple without a priest? How could such a thing be?" asked the priest. Tasuke did not reply.

"Indeed," the great man continued, "I am the priest here, and have been for quite some time."

Tasuke was suspicious. Perhaps the old woman had been mocking him. But she had given him such a fine bowl full of food he found it hard to doubt her. No, something was wrong with the priest. Something more than his great size — something that Tasuke could not define clearly — something was wrong about the priest.

"Coming to the point of my sudden visit, I would like to impose upon the hospitality of the temple for the night, with your permission. Tomorrow I will continue on my travels."

"By all means, please stay." The priest laughed a deep, hearty laugh. "Stay longer if you like. It isn't often I am blessed with guests."

The priest showed Tasuke to the common room of the temple, where he indicated the monk was to make his bed. Goro brought food and the two warmed themselves before a fire in a hearth built in the center of the room. The smoke from the fire curled lazily up to the high ceiling of the room, where it escaped through a vent and filtered out into the night.

The priest asked Tasuke for the latest news from his travels, and the two discussed this and other matters late into the night. The priest pushed Tasuke, asking countless questions on a given topic until he was satisfied and moved on to the next topic.

This relentless questioning in the guise of conversation soon took a great toll of Tasuke, who began to feel sleepy. Seeing this, his host began making preparations for bed. But before taking his leave he seated himself again before the crackling fire.

"You have traveled a great deal, monk Tasuke. And you have no doubt learned many things."

"Only those that were revealed to me," replied Tasuke.

"Oh, come now. Show me some of your talents, some of your skills. Shall we have a contest?"

"Would it not be rude to compete with my host?" asked the traveler.

"Perhaps, but it would be a greater rudeness to fail to oblige your host with a simple demonstration of skills."

"Ah," said Tasuke. "Very well. A contest it shall be."

Tasuke cleared away the bedding that had been set out for him and the two sat facing each other before the hearth.

"Though it may be rude for me, the guest, to insist on following the host, I would like to allow you to show your skills first."

"Indeed," answered the priest. "But surely you have seen many wondrous things in the course of your travels. I only hope I do not disappoint you."

"First, I will become a giant," said the priest. No sooner had the words left his lips than the priest's body grew and grew until he was almost twelve feet in height.

Tasuke was unimpressed. "That is what you wanted to show me?"

The priest sucked his teeth and told the monk, "No, I can grow even larger." Then he began growing again until his head brushed the ceiling.

"How is this?" he asked the traveler.

Tasuke did not look up at his host. Keeping his gaze level, he answered, "That is indeed impressive. But I can do that and better with ease."

He paused to let his words have their effect. "But what's really difficult is to make yourself smaller."

The priest drew in a great breath and made himself smaller, reducing himself to about three feet in height.

Tasuke belittled his host. "Child's play, if I may be so rude." The priest then made himself smaller until he was scarcely the size of a persimmon seed. Seeing this, Tasuke grabbed the soft rice cake the woman had given him. Quickly, he slammed the cake down on the pea-sized priest. The soft, sticky rice cake enveloped the priest and held him fast.

The monk put the rice cake on a wire grill and set it over the fire. The cake began to crackle and smoulder until there was a great shriek and the priest broke free. Still no larger than a pea and badly burned by the fire, he jumped from the grill to the floor. There he resumed his true form, that of a weasel, and fled the temple, never to be seen again.

As dawn approached, the old woman led a group of townspeople to the temple to see what had become of the young priest. Rather than another body with its throat ripped out, they found the priest digging in the garden. Surprised, they asked him how he had avoided the fate that had befallen so many others.

"The old woman gave me a clue as to how it was done," Tasuke recounted. "She said all the priests had their throats torn as if by some animal.

"When I came here, I found a priest was already here. We talked late into the night until he challenged me to a demonstration of skills, whereupon he grew like a giant until he was nearly twenty feet tall.

"It was then that I realized that if I looked up at him in surprise, I would expose my throat to him. Had I looked up, you would have found my torn body here this morning. Fortunately, I have triumphed over the evil."

The townspeople rejoiced that their temple was free from the murderous monster that had troubled them for so long. They embraced Tasuke with open arms when he volunteered to stay at the temple and become their priest.

Kachi-kachi-yama

THE old man set out for his fields with his hoe on his shoulder. The soil of the Rikuchū part of northern Japan had been good to him, though the years had not been easy. The man worked hard, turning the soil and planting beans in his field. As he worked, he sang a nonsense tune to himself:

One little bean grows into a thousand,
I plant two beans,
I get two thousand,
Then we will eat happily,
For years and years and years.

The man was so wrapped up in his work he did not hear the *rustle*rustle*rustle* as a badger wandered out from the woods nearby. The badger sat down made himself comfortable on a broad rock where he sunned himself for a while before turning his attention to the farmer. The badger began teasing the man, singing to the same tune as the farmer had:

Swing that hoe, old man, swing that hoe.
Grow me some tasty crops to eat this year.

You plant one bean, I eat nine hundred.
Swing that hoe, old man, swing that hoe.
Swing that hoe and sweat some more.

The farmer was normally a good-natured man, but he was outraged at the badger's audacity. That the very creature that stole the fruit of the man's labors would come to him and brag about it was too much for the man to endure. He raised his hoe and charged across the field toward the badger.

"Woah, old man," cried the badger as he turned tail and fled up the mountain. "Is it really this easy to get you angry?"

The next day the farmer returned to his fields and continued clearing and planting his fields. Again, the badger rustled out from the woods and sat down on the warm, flat rock, where he began teasing the old man once more.

*How about some better crops this year,
     old man?
Last year's harvest was good, old man,
But I know you can do better this year.
Swing that hoe some more, old man.
Swing that hoe for me some more.*

The man lost his temper and once again raised his hoe to chase the badger into the woods. The badger easily eluded him, and soon disappeared among the brambles and thickets, leaving the man alone at the edge of his field. Walking back to his field, the man wondered what to do about the pest.

"If I don't do anything," he thought, "he will be back every day to bother me while I work. Then, when the crops are ready, he'll take half my crops before I can harvest them. What can I do to stop him?"

The man thought about his problem all the while he worked in his fields. By the time the day's work was done, he had decided on a plan.

The next day, the man went to his fields as usual. Before beginning his work, however, he went to the broad rock where the badger liked to sun himself. Working quickly, he painted the rock thoroughly with a thick coat of a strong, clear glue. Then he went about working in his fields as before.

As before, the badger came out from the

woods. He went to the broad rock and, not noticing the glue on it, sat down and stretched out in the sun. After a few moments of sunbathing, he began, as before, teasing the farmer.

> *I hope you got a good night's sleep last night.*
> *I hope you give it your all today.*
> *Swing that hoe, old man,*
> *Swing that hoe for me.*

The man looked up from his work and spoke to the badger. "You're back, I see. Well, you are a vile little rodent." He continued speaking as he began walking very slowly toward the badger. "Oh, dear. Is that right? Are badgers rodents? In any case, you are a vile fellow."

The man grabbed a handful of wisteria vines from the path beside the field and continued walking slowly toward the badger. The badger tried to make his escape into the fields as he had before. This time, however, he found himself stuck fast to the rock. He wriggled and writhed, trying to free himself, but there was no escape. The badger could not move from the rock.

The old man teased the badger as he approached.

> *Mister Badger, you're done for,*
> *You'll tease me no more,*
> *I'll work very hard tomorrow*
> *After Badger Stew tonight.*

The man used the wisteria vines as ropes, which he then tied around the badger. Slinging the badger over his shoulder, the happy farmer and went home.

"Obāchan, obāchan!" he called from the doorway to his modest home. "Heat up the kettle! Badger Stew for supper tonight!"

No one answered, so the farmer went into the kitchen, where he hung the badger from a hook in the ceiling. The farmer pulled at the vines binding the badger and, satisfied they would hold, he went off to the village to buy ingredients for badger stew.

The farmer's wife was in the garden pounding rice into *mochi*. All alone, she pounded the rice with a special hammer. The *tok-shikki-pah, tok-shikki-pah* of the hammer made so much noise she did not hear her husband when he returned with his catch.

After a while, the farmer's wife put down the hammer and went into the kitchen for a break.

"Obāsan?"

The woman was startled to hear an unfamiliar voice call her name from within her very own kitchen. She looked about the kitchen in a surprise. Seeing nothing, her surprise turned to fear.

"Up here," said the voice.

The woman looked up and saw the badger, tied up and hanging from the ceiling.

The badger moved to capitalize on the woman surprise before she could regain her composure. "You look tired. That's pretty tough work, huh? Pounding *mochi*?"

"Yes," answered the woman, not at all sure of what to say.

"Do you think you could get me down from here? It's really uncomfortable, you know."

"How did you get up there in the first place?"

The badger ignored her question. "I could help you with the *mochi*. Badgers are pretty strong, you know."

The woman did not reply.

"You're making *mochi* for your husband, right? That's really sweet. You must care for him a lot."

The woman nodded.

"You must have a thousand other things to do besides pound *mochi*. I could do that for you and it wouldn't take half the time it would take you. And you could do those thousand other things — or you could rest up a little bit. As long as the *mochi* get pounded, no one will ever know who did the pounding, right?"

The tired woman found this appealing, and she untied the smooth-talking badger and handed him the hammer.

The badger took the hammer and began pounding *mochi* with a *tok-shikki-pah, tok-shikki-pah*. The old woman sat down to rest for a moment, but the moment she turned her back on the badger he crept up behind her. Swinging the hammer with all his might, he struck her in the head and killed her.

The badger quickly assumed the old woman's shape. His transformation was so complete not even her husband would be able to tell that the shape-changing badger was not really his wife.

Next, he found the old couple's kettle and began making a big pot of Old Woman Stew.

"Yaa, it's so cold out," said the old man to his wife on his return.

"I've made some nice warm soup for you," said the woman. "Here, sit down and have some."

The old man sat at the table and his wife brought him a bowl filled with a meaty soup.

"Are you feeling well? Your voice sounds wrong," said the farmer.

"Wrong? No, no. I think I'm catching a cold. I was very busy today, you know, pounding *mochi* and so on. I'm pretty tired."

Hungry from the day's work and happy with the way things had gone, the man tried a mouthful of the stew. "The meat's a bit tough. Did you overcook it?"

"Of course not. It must have been an old badger, that's all."

The old couple ate their meal and went to bed.

The badger awoke the next morning before dawn, whereupon he whispered cruelly to the sleeping old man:

Old Woman Stew,
Mmmm, mmmm good, don'tcha know.
It's probably still stuck between your teeth, hunh?
See the burned kimono in the garden,
And the happy dogs with fresh bones.

The badger fled back up the mountain just as the man awoke with a start. He had had this awful dream, he told his wife, that the badger they had eaten for supper had somehow changed places with her, killing her and serving her for supper instead. When his wife did not reply, the man bolted from his bed to the garden, where he found the charred remains of his wife's *kimono*. On the porch, the old couple's dog slept contentedly with a very long bone tucked under its forepaws.

"IIIYYYAAAAAAAaaaaaaaaaaa!!!" The man's cry of misery drifted across the valley like a slow, rolling fog.

Hearing the old man's moan, a hare came

rushing to see what had happened. "What's the matter old man? Why did you scream just now?"

"A badger killed my wife," sobbed the man. "Then he served her up as stew — and I ate her without knowing it. Oh, what a miserable wretch I am..."

The rabbit comforted the man, then swore to help him. "I can't bring your wife back, but I promise she will be avenged. Stop crying, and I will return to you as soon as the badger has met his fate." With that, the hare hopped off to the mountains to find the badger.

The hare headed to a meadow of old, brown reeds, where he began cutting reeds with his teeth. The noise drew the badger's attention, and he soon came rustling through the reeds to see what was going on.

"Hare!" he called. "What are you doing cutting reeds?"

"This winter is going to be a cold one, so I want to build a hut with these reeds and spend the winter inside it."

"Really? That sounds like a good idea! If I help, can I spend the winter there too?"

"Sure," said the hare. "That sounds great."

The badger joined the hare and soon the two had cut a great pile of reeds.

"Alright," said the hare. "We'll be safer from humans if we build the hut higher up the mountain. Let's bundle these reeds together and carry them up the trail."

The two tied as many reeds as they could

carry into a bundle. "Here, let me get that," said the hare as he helped the badger load a great bundle of reeds onto a back. "It'll be safer if I tie the bundle to your back — it won't fall off that way." The badger agreed, and the hare tied the bundle tightly to his back.

"Okay, you go first."

The badger set out up the trail with the hare a few steps behind. After a few minutes, the hare called to the badger is a tired voice, "How are you doing? Is it too heavy for you?"

"Not at all," answered the badger, proud of his strength. "I could carry this forever."

"Great, great." The hare was only pretending to sound tired, as he was not carrying a load of reeds after all. The badger, with an enormous bundle of reeds on his back, could not turn around and see that the hare was following him with only two stones in his hands. The stones were flints, and the hare used them to light a small fire when he stopped along the trail. He set a small bundle of reeds alight, then tossed that bundle on top of the great bundle strapped to the badger's back.

The fire smouldered at first, then came to life with a *kachi-kachi* crackling sound.

"What's that crackling sound," asked the badger. "Do you hear it? It sounds like *kachi-kachi, kachi-kachi*."

"This is *Kachi-kachi* Mountain," said the hare. "It gets its name from the *kachi-kachi* bird. It must be the bird that you hear. Ah! I hear it too!"

The badger acknowledged this and continued up the path.

The hare leaned over closer to the small fire and blew on it (*fuu-fuu*) to encourage it to grow. The badger, with keen hearing, heard this *fuu-fuu* sound as well, and asked the hare about it.

"The *fuu-fuu* bird is said to live on this mountain as well. I hear it too, but it sounds pretty far away."

The badger stopped and strained his ears to listen to the song of the *fuu-fuu* bird. Then he continued along the path.

By now, the fire was growing larger, leaping to life with a roaring *raa-raa* sound.

Again, the badger asked the hare about the sound, and again, the hare was able to tell him that the sound was that of some exotic wild bird: the *raa-raa* bird.

The flames quickly grew to consume the whole bundle of reeds. "Hare, hare, put it out! Put out the fire!" screamed the badger, but the hare had disappeared down the mountain.

The next day the hare went up a neighboring mountain covered with snakeweeds, bushes and other dense brush. The hare spent the morning gathering tasty snakeweeds and leaves, which it then ate. With a full tummy, the hare fell fast asleep under a great tree.

"You!"

The hare woke with a start to find angry face of the badger before him. His back was red and terribly burned by the fire, but he was still alive.

The badger was standing over him. There was no escape.

"You, hare," roared the badger. "What a horrible thing you did to me yesterday on the mountain of reeds! I should kill you right here and now, but I want to make you suffer. I'm not sure yet how I'll kill you, but I know I'll make it last a long, long — "

"Excuse me," the hare said meekly. "You seem to have me confused with another hare. I am the hare of Snakeweed Mountain. I think you want the hare of Reed Mountain."

"Eh? Snakeweed Mountain? Reed? What are you on about?"

"I'm sure that's it. That character on Reed Mountain gives all us hares a bad name, you know. Telling tall tales, playing pranks on other creatures of the wood. He's no good, I tell you, no good."

"I KNOW that," bellowed the angry badger. "Look what he did to me."

The badger turned to show the hare his disfigured back. There were lines where the ropes holding the bundle of reeds to his back had been.

"It's not enough that he goes and tries to kill me. Winter's coming and he has to burn my winter coat in some stupid prank. When I catch him I'll, I'll . . . Rarrrrrrr!!!"

The badger clawed at the earth in anger while the hare moved to the side.

The badger gradually calmed down and sat down in front of the hare. "Snakeweed Mountain, huh? And you eat snakeweeds?"

"Yes, I do. They're pretty tasty," said the hare, patting his tummy, "but they're even better as medicine for burns."

"Burns? You don't say? The pain in my back is killing me. Do you think you could put some of them on my back for me?"

"Sure. Any enemy of that rascal on Reed Mountain is a friend of mine. But I must warn you — snakeweed will heal your burns after a while, but it will hurt like the devil when I first put it on."

"Anything, anything. Just as long as the pain goes away and I can grow my coat back."

"Okay," said the hare. "But don't lose your temper when it hurts."

The hare gathered up a bundle of snakeweeds and had the badger grind them into a powder, to which the hare added some water, producing a thick snakeweed paste.

"Okay, it's ready" said the hare. He told the badger to turn around, then added, "No matter how much it hurts, you musn't try to take the paste off until it dries. And whatever you do, don't get it wet."

The badger agreed and the hare, with the badger's back turned to him, added ground red pepper to the paste. Ignoring the burned smell emanating from the badger, the hare applied the paste generously to the badger's badly burned back.

"Yaaaa!!!" cried the badger. "It hurts, hare, it hurts!"

"Endure it for a little while and it will get better."

But the badger could only endure the paste for a short while. He jumped to his feet and ran down to the mountain to a lake. Then, remembering the hare's warning, he hesitated, wondering how much worse it would be if he dove into the lake and washed the paste off. While the badger writhed in both pain and indecision, the hare made his escape down another path.

The next day, the hare was on a mountain of pine trees, making a snack of some pine bark, when suddenly the badger appeared before him.

"It's over, hare!" he yelled.

The hare, startled, did his best to look surprised.

"Over? Why? What has — what happened to your back?"

"You know darned good and well, hare. It's

all your doing! And now you're going to pay!"

"No, no. I've done nothing," said the hare. "I've been here all the while. I have witnesses, too!" The hare looked around. "Well, they were here. They'll be back. But I assure you, I have been here for days."

The badger calmed down a bit, and the hare took the opportunity to ask, "How did you get that pasty mess on your back? That looks like — hey, that's snakeweed, isn't it? On burns? I thought everybody knew snakeweed was one of the worst things you could put on a burn! That just makes it hurt worse! And pepper! Who did this to you badger?"

The badger began to believe the hare before him was indeed a different hare, and told him the tale of the hares of Reed and Snakeweed Mountains.

"Why didn't you jump into a lake to get that paste off you?" the hare asked innocently.

The badger growled a low, rumbling growl and looked away.

"Fear not, friend badger. As a wise old badger like you should be able to guess by taking a look around you, I am the hare of Pine Mountain. I'm gathering clay and mud now to make a boat."

"A boat? Why?"

"This is going to be one tough winter this year, and I think we're going to need all the food we can get our paws on. The lake down there — you know, the big one — is full of fish, which means it's full of food for us during the winter months. But the best fish are in the deepest part of the lake, and we need boats to get there."

"I see," said the badger. "That sounds like a good plan. Would you mind if I join you?"

"Not at all," answered the hare. "The more the merrier. Ah, but there's only enough mud for one boat."

"Oh?"

"That's no problem. I'll let you have all the mud for your boat. Pine will do just as well, so I'll make my boat out of pine."

With the hare's guidance, the two animals build their boats and set them on the water. The hare's boat floated easily on the surface, but the badger's clay boat drooped sadly the moment it entered the water.

"What would you say to a race?" proposed the hare. "Whoever gets to the center of the lake first wins."

"Would that be fair?" asked the badger. "I mean, after all, you let me have the better boat."

"True, you have the clay boat, while mine is made from pine. And you're stronger than me, so you have two advantages. Still, I like a challenge. Let's do it!"

The badger agreed and the two set out on the lake. The hare had no trouble guiding his craft toward the center of the great lake, but he made a great show of pretending it was difficult to keep up with the badger. As the pair neared the center of the lake, however, the hare overtook the badger.

KACHI-KACHI-YAMA 153

The badger, concentrating on the race, did not notice his clay boat was slowly melting away in the water. By the time the badger did notice, the hare was far away.

"Hare! Hare!" cried the badger. "Something is wrong with my boat. It's falling apart in the water!"

The hare, who by this time was no more than a tiny speck on the badger's horizon, pretended not to hear the badger's cries. He waved at the badger, as if teasing him for being so slow.

Meanwhile, the badger struggled helplessly as his boat disintegrated beneath him. Unable to swim, he soon disappeared beneath the waves and was never seen again.

The hare returned to the old farmer's home and told him his tale. The farmer cried when he learned his wife's death had been avenged, and he thanked the hare profusely. He racked his brain trying to find a way to thank the hare for his help, when suddenly the thought came to him.

"Would you," he asked the hare, "consider living with me? I can keep you warm in the winter, and you'll have food all round — especially now that that badger won't be stealing half my crops."

The hare agreed, and the two lived the remaining years of their lives together in the valley of Kachi-kachi Mountain.